RENEW YOUR WORSHIP

D1365393

RENEW YOUR WORSHIP

A Study in the Blending of
Traditional and Contemporary Worship

Robert E. Webber

The Alleluia! Series of the Institute for Worship Studies

HENDRICKSON
PUBLISHERS

Hendrickson Publishers, Inc.
P.O. Box 3473
Peabody, Massachusetts 01961-3473

RENEW YOUR WORSHIP:
A Study in the Blending of Traditional and Contemporary Worship
by Robert E. Webber

ISBN 1-56563-256-7

Third printing, March 2005

Printed in the United States of America

CONTENTS

WELCOME TO THE
ALLELUIA! SERIES

This Bible study series has been designed by the Institute for Worship Studies primarily for laypersons in the church.

We are living in a time when worship has become a distinct priority for the church. For years, the church has emphasized evangelism, teaching, fellowship, missions, and service to society to the neglect of the very source of its power—worship. But in recent years we have witnessed a Spirit-led renewal in the study and practice of worship.

Because worship has been neglected for so many years, there is precious little information and teaching on the subject in our seminaries, Bible schools, and local churches.

The mission of the Institute for Worship Studies is to make the study of worship available to everyone in the church—academician, pastor, worship leader, music minister, and layperson.

Laypersons will find the seven courses of the Alleluia! Series to be inspiring, informative, and life changing. Each course of study is rooted in biblical teaching, draws from the rich historical treasures of the church, and is highly practical and accessible.

The Institute for Worship Studies presents this course, *Renew Your Worship: A Study in the Blending of Traditional and Contemporary Worship,* as a service to the local church and to its ministry of worship to God. May this study warm your heart, inform your mind, and kindle your spirit. May it inspire and set on fire the worship of the local church. And may this study minister to the church and to the One, Holy, Triune God in whose name it is offered.

THE SEVEN COURSES IN THE ALLELUIA! WORSHIP SERIES

Learning to Worship with All Your Heart: A Study in the Biblical Foundations of Worship

You are led into the rich teachings of worship in both the Old and the New Testaments. Learn the vocabulary of worship, be introduced to theological themes, and study various descriptions of worship. Each lesson inspires you to worship at a deeper level—from the inside out.

Rediscovering the Missing Jewel: A Study of Worship through the Centuries

This stretching course introduces you to the actual worship styles of Christians in other centuries and geographical locations. Study the history of the early, medieval, Reformation, modern, and contemporary periods of worship. Learn from them how your worship today may be enriched, inspired, and renewed. Each lesson introduces you to rich treasures of worship adaptable for contemporary use.

Renew Your Worship! A Study in the Blending of Traditional and Contemporary Worship

This inspiring course leads you into a deeper understanding and experience of your Sunday worship. How does worship bring the congregation into the presence of God, mold the people by the Word, and feed the believers spiritually? The answer to these and other questions will bring a new spiritual depth to your experience of worship.

Enter His Courts with Praise: A Study of the Role of Music and the Arts in Worship

This course introduces you to the powerful way the arts can communicate the mystery of God at work in worship. Music, visual arts, drama, dance, and mime are seen as means through which the gospel challenges the congregation and changes lives.

Rediscovering the Christian Feasts: A Study in the Services of the Christian Year

This stimulating and stretching course helps you experience the traditional church calendar with new eyes. It challenges the secular concept of time and shows how the practice of the Christian year offers an alternative to secularism and shapes the Christian's day-to-day experience of time, using the gospel as its grid.

Encountering the Healing Power of God: A Study in the Sacred Actions of Worship

This course makes a powerful plea for the recovery of those sacred actions that shape the spiritual life. Baptism, Communion, anointing with oil, and other sacred actions are all interpreted with reflection on the death and resurrection of Jesus. These actions shape the believer's spiritual experience into a continual pattern of death to sin and rising to life in the Spirit.

Empowered by the Holy Spirit: A Study in the Ministries of Worship

This course will challenge you to see the relationship between worship and life in the secular world. It empowers the believer in evangelism, spiritual formation, social action, care ministries, and other acts of love and charity.

Take all seven courses and earn a Certificate of Worship Studies (CWS). For more information, call the Institute for Worship Studies at (630) 510-8905.

INTRODUCTION

Renew Your Worship: A Study in the Blending of Traditional and Contemporary Worship may be used for personal study or a small-group course of study and spiritual formation. It is designed around thirteen easy-to-understand sessions. Each session has a two-part study guide. The first part is an individual study that each person completes privately. The second part is a one-hour interaction and application session that group members complete together (during the week or in an adult Sunday school setting). The first part helps you recall and reflect on what you've read, while the small-group study applies the material to each member's personal life and experience of public worship.

Renew Your Worship is designed for use by one or more people. When the course is used in a group setting, the person who is designated as the leader simply needs to lead the group through the lesson step by step. It is always best to choose a leader before you begin.

Here are some suggestions for making your group discussions lively and insightful.

SUGGESTIONS FOR THE STUDENT

A few simple guidelines will help you use the study guide most effectively. They can be summarized under three headings: Prepare, Participate, and Apply.

Prepare

1. Answer each question in the study guide, "Part I: Personal Study," thoughtfully and critically.

2. Do all your work prayerfully. Prayer itself is worship. As you increase your knowledge of worship, do so in a spirit of prayerful openness before God.

Participate

1. Don't be afraid to ask questions. Your questions may give voice to the other members in the group. Your courage in speaking out will give others permission to talk and may encourage more stimulating discussion.

2. Don't hesitate to share your personal experiences. Abstract thinking has its place, but personal illustrations will help you and others remember the material more vividly.

3. Be open to others. Listen to the stories that other members tell, and respond to them in a way that does not invalidate their experiences.

Apply

1. Always ask yourself, "How can this apply to worship?"

2. Commit yourself to being a more intentional worshiper. Involve yourself in what is happening around you.

3. Determine your gifts. Ask yourself, "What can I do in worship that will minister to the body of Christ?" Then offer your gifts and talents to worship.

SUGGESTIONS FOR THE LEADER

Like the worship that it advocates, the group study in *Renew Your Worship* is dialogic in nature. Because this study has been developed around the principles of discussion and sharing, a monologue or lecture approach will not work. The following guidelines will help you encourage discussion, facilitate learning, and implement the practice of worship. Use these guidelines with "Part II: Group Discussion" in each session.

1. Encourage the participants to prepare thoroughly and to bring their Bibles and study guides to each session.

2. Begin each session with prayer. Since worship is a kind of prayer, learning about worship should be a prayerful experience.

3. Discuss each question individually. Ask for several answers and encourage people to react to comments made by others.

4. Use a chalkboard or flip chart or dry-erase board. Draw charts and symbols that visually enhance the ideas being presented. Outline major concepts.

5. Look for practical applications of answers and suggestions that are offered. Try asking questions like, "How would you include this in our worship?" "How would you feel about that change?" "How does this insight help you to be a better worshiper?"

6. Invite concrete personal illustrations. Ask questions like, "Have you experienced that? Where? When? Describe how you felt in that particular situation."

7. When you have concluded Session 9, send the names and addresses of all the students who will complete the class to: Institute for Worship Studies, Box 894, Wheaton, IL 60189. We will then send a certificate of accomplishment for each student in time for you to distribute them during the last class. The cost of each certificate is $1.00. (Add $3.00 for postage and handling.)

One final suggestion: Purchase the larger work upon which this course is based, volume 3 of *The Complete Library of Christian Worship*. This volume, entitled *The Renewal of Sunday Worship*, contains an in-depth study of worship renewal. It is a beautiful 8½-by-11-inch coffee table book that will inform your mind and inspire your heart through hours of reading and study.

PART I

WHY

SUNDAY

WORSHIP?

WHAT IS WORSHIP RENEWAL?

A Study in the Signs of a Renewing Worship

 Participatory worship—to achieve it, we must break through the barriers of passive worship. Coming to an understanding of worship renewal will help us move toward our goal.

THE NEED FOR WORSHIP RENEWAL

I first became aware of the need for worship renewal in my local church in the late sixties. I was involved in a church that I could best describe as formal and distant. While my best friends were in this church, friends that I clicked with on a personal and social basis, there was something lacking when we gathered together for the purpose of worship. Inexplicably, the camaraderie, the animation, the joy that we experienced when we did things together were lost when we assembled for worship.

I'm not sure that I can put my finger on what was wrong. I only know that *something* was amiss. How is it, I asked myself, that this same community of people can have so much fun at a church outing, a church picnic, a potluck dinner, or social gatherings in the home, but become so rigid, so lifeless, so formal and cold when gathered for worship?

SIGNS OF A WORSHIP IN RENEWAL

I left the church that I just described and went in search of a church with a renewed worship. Because I couldn't find what I wanted, I joined with several like-minded people to begin a home church that met in my house. (I'm not recommending that you do this.)

Our goal was to get as close as possible to the early church experience of worship. We wanted a comfortable and casual atmosphere, we wanted to include the children in an experience that would be enjoyable and life changing, we wanted sermons that were relevant to our needs, and we wanted to celebrate the feast of the Lord's table weekly.

We did all of these things and found a great enjoyment in our worship. Our little house-church experiment ended two years later when we all returned to established churches seeking the renewal of worship in communities of faith that had connections with historic Christianity. Nevertheless, as I have reflected on my experience in the home church, I have been able to think more clearly about the subject of a renewed worship.

DEFINING WORSHIP

I'm convinced that worship renewal is ultimately a gift of the Spirit, a gift for which we need to pray. But I also think we can exercise our will and our mind as we approach worship renewal. I've found, for example, that it is really helpful to establish a definition of worship.

Most people don't seem to be aware that worship begins with God, not with us. A lot of people seem to think that worship is exclusively what the people do. What they miss is that worship begins with God. In worship God does what God has done in history. That is, God comes to us. God initiates a relationship with us in worship. Our job is to respond, to be open to God, to receive God's work in us and for us.

The shortest, perhaps the best, definition of worship I have ever heard is the simple statement that "worship is a celebration of God's mighty deed of salvation in Jesus Christ."

In this definition we can see two things at work. First, God speaks and acts through the proclamation and enactment of the divine saving deeds. Second, we respond to these deeds with praise and worship.

Worship renewal, then, is the celebration of God's saving deeds that results in a much clearer sense of the power of the gospel at work in the assembly of people who have gathered to worship. It is also the reception of God's power in our own lives as the gospel takes root in us through our receptivity. The result is a congregation of people who continually experience the power of God in their lives—a power that brings healing and empowers their lives and ministry.

OPENNESS TO CHANGE

I am convinced that worship renewal cannot happen in the local church unless that church and its people are really and truly open to change. Unfortunately, many churches are very divided over the issue of worship renewal. Let me give you an example.

About ten years ago, I decided I needed a year of experience leading worship in a local church, so I thought really hard about where I could get this kind of experience. Finally, I chose a church that had a reputation for being progressive and forward looking.

I called the pastor and said, "I'd like to offer my services to your church as worship coordinator for a full year. Would you be interested in letting me work with your congregation and experiment in worship renewal? It would give me the experience I need and it would give your church the opportunity to move toward worship renewal. It could be a win/win situation for both of us."

The pastor, an acquaintance of mine, responded favorably right away. But he said, "I've got to get this passed through my board."

The proposal was presented and the board, not certain they wanted to do this, asked me to come and talk to them.

Our meeting was not a pleasant experience. The first question was asked by an angry person, "Don't we worship here? What makes you think we need worship renewal?" This very closed-minded person dominated the discussion, killed the proposal, and persuaded the board not to let me come.

The point is clear. A church that is not open to change will probably not experience worship renewal. On the other hand, the church open to change is good soil for the seeds of renewal.

CONCLUSION

In this session we have explored the question, What is worship renewal? This is a very difficult and involved question that cannot be addressed in a superficial manner. It requires (1) an understanding of a worship in need of renewal, (2) a good grasp of the signs of a renewing worship, (3) an understanding of worship as a celebration of God's saving deeds, and (4) an openness on the part of the church to the renewal of its worship.

STUDY GUIDE

Read Session 1, "What Is Worship Renewal?"
before starting the study guide.

PART I: PERSONAL STUDY

Answer the following questions on your own.

1. *Life Connection*

◆ Was there a point in your life when you first became aware of a need for worship renewal? In the space below tell the story of that experience.

_____

_____

_____

_____

_____

2. *Content Questions*

◆ Below is a list of fourteen signs of a church that needs worship renewal. If a statement describes your church, check yes. If it does not, check no.

1. The congregation is passive and lacking in enthusiasm and a spirit of joy. ❑ Yes ❑ No

2. Visitors do not feel welcome or drawn into the community and its worship. ❑ Yes ❑ No

3. Worship is cerebral and oriented almost exclusively toward teaching. ❑ Yes ❑ No

4. Worship is evangelistic and oriented almost exclusively toward conversion. ❑ Yes ❑ No

5. Communication skills in preaching and leading worship are weak. ❑ Yes ❑ No

6. Sermons tend to be long, didactic, and lacking in application. ❑ Yes ❑ No

7. Communion is celebrated infrequently and when celebrated seems to be tacked on to the end of the service, often bearing the characteristics of a funeral. ❑ Yes ❑ No

8. People sit in a typical classroom formation with the back of another person's head as a major object of sight. ❑ Yes ❑ No

9. Singing lacks life, and the range of music is limited. ❑ Yes ❑ No

10. There is no sense in which the order of worship moves the congregation in a pattern that rehearses their faith and thus establishes, maintains, or repairs a relationship with God. ❑ Yes ❑ No

11. The Christian year is not practiced, or if it is practiced, it is not characterized by a sense of its gospel nature or used effectively as a means of ordering congregational spirituality. ❑ Yes ❑ No

12. The use of arts is shunned except on special occasions such as Christmas or Easter. ❑ Yes ❑ No

13. The people are not involved in responses, antiphons, prayer, ministry to each other, or the passing of the peace. ❑ Yes ❑ No

14. The senses are not adequately engaged in touch, smell, sight, or hearing. ❑ Yes ❑ No

• Below is a list of twenty-one signs of a church that is experiencing the renewal of worship. If a statement describes your church, check yes. If it does not, check no.

1. Restoration of a Christ-centered focus (worship celebrates the living, dying, and rising of Christ in which the powers of evil are overthrown, a sacrifice for sin is made, and an example for living is set forth) ❑ Yes ❑ No

2. Characterized by a good balance of order and freedom ❑ Yes ❑ No

3. Rediscovery of Christ's active presence in both word and table ❑ Yes ❑ No

4. Appropriation of the arts as servants of the text   ❑ Yes ❑ No

5. Use of a wide range of music drawn from the history   ❑ Yes ❑ No
    of the church and from various contemporary cul-
    tures

6. Heightened communication skills in both preach-   ❑ Yes ❑ No
    ing and leading of worship

7. A space for worship that works for the participation   ❑ Yes ❑ No
    of all the people

8. A worship that is intergenerational   ❑ Yes ❑ No

9. A worship characterized by intimacy and pageantry   ❑ Yes ❑ No

10. A warm and hospitable environment   ❑ Yes ❑ No

11. Rediscovery of the evangelical nature of the church   ❑ Yes ❑ No
    year

12. Aliveness of the people through active participation   ❑ Yes ❑ No

13. An experience of joy, celebration, love, victory, and   ❑ Yes ❑ No
    peace

14. A rehearsal of one's relationship to God   ❑ Yes ❑ No

15. The engagement of the whole person—mind, heart,   ❑ Yes ❑ No
    will, body, and senses

16. The experience of spontaneity   ❑ Yes ❑ No

17. A feeling of personal involvement and corporate   ❑ Yes ❑ No
    relatedness

18. The ministry of people to one another in worship   ❑ Yes ❑ No

19. A growing concern for and commitment to evangel-   ❑ Yes ❑ No
    ism and social outreach

20. A heightened spirituality, both personal and corpo-   ❑ Yes ❑ No
    rate

21. The experience of Christian community   ❑ Yes ❑ No

◆ How do you respond to the definition of worship used in this session ("Worship is a celebration of God's mighty deeds of salvation in Jesus Christ")?_____

_____

_____

_____

_____

◆ Explain both the divine and the human aspects of this definition of worship:

_____

_____

_____

_____

_____

◆ Define "worship renewal." _____

_____

_____

_____

_____

_____

3. *Application*

◆ Read and think about the answers you gave to the statements above describing the fourteen signs of a worshiping community that needs worship renewal. Would you say that your church needs worship renewal? ❑ Yes ❑ No   Explain: _____

_____

_____

_____

_____

_____

♦ Look again at the fourteen signs of apathetic worship. Name what you think are the three most severe problems or impediments to worship renewal that your church faces.

a. _____
_____
_____

b. _____
_____
_____

c. _____
_____
_____

♦ What can your church do to overcome these problems? Comment on each of the three issues identified above:

a. _____
_____

b. _____
_____

c. _____
_____

♦ What one characteristic of a renewing worship would you *most* like to see recovered in your worship? Choose one from the list of twenty-one characteristics of a renewed worship. _____
_____
_____

♦ How would you go about restoring this aspect of renewed worship in your local church? _____
_____
_____
_____
_____
_____

PART II: GROUP DISCUSSION

Write all of the group members' answers to the questions in each section on a chalkboard or flip chart.

1. *Life Connection*

   ◆ Begin the group study by asking several members of the group to share the experience that first made them aware of the need for worship renewal.

2. *Thought Questions*

   ◆ Walk through the fourteen signs of a church in need of worship renewal. Poll the group to find out how many were answered yes and how many were answered no. Encourage a discussion on the questions of greatest importance to the group.

   ◆ Walk through the signs of a church experiencing the renewal of worship. Poll the group to find out how many were answered no and how many were answered yes. Encourage a discussion on the questions of greater importance to the group.

   ◆ Ask for a response to the brief definition of worship used in this chapter: "Worship is a celebration of God's mighty deeds of salvation in Jesus Christ."

   ◆ Ask, "How do you define worship renewal?"

3. *Application*

   ◆ How did each student answer the question, Would you say that your church needs worship renewal?

   ◆ Ask the students to comment on the three impediments to worship renewal in their church. Is there general agreement?

   ◆ Encourage the students to talk about how these impediments may be overcome.

   ◆ What is the *one* characteristic of worship renewal that each student would most like to see recovered in worship? Is there any agreement?

   ◆ Ask, "How would you go about restoring this aspect of renewal worship in your local church?"

WHAT IS WORSHIP ALL ABOUT?
A Study in the Definition of Worship

 A number of years ago, when I first began to feel a growing interest in worship, the pastor of my church announced that he was going to teach a series on worship in the adult Sunday school class.

I don't know how you feel when the pastor announces that he or she will address a matter that is of utmost importance to you. I only remember that I greeted the announcement with great enthusiasm and then went to the class with an unusual amount of anticipation. Perhaps you have approached this or that class with an expectation similar to mine, so you know what I'm talking about.

Well, I have to tell you I was most disappointed. I felt I never came to grasp the meaning of worship, possibly because the pastor didn't understand it and because the subject was so vast.

Actually, this disappointing experience proved to have a positive side. I realized the problem wasn't so much that the pastor was unprepared, but that worship was a vast and mysterious subject that demanded a lifetime of attention.

That was more than twenty years ago. I am still pursuing the subject, with no end in sight. I now believe, as the minister said, "Worship, like God, is a mystery that can never be exhausted."

In this brief study we are going to look at the subject of worship, but with the realization that what we say and study touches on a vast and unconquerable subject. What we can grasp is only a beginning.

WORSHIP EXTOLS THE CHARACTER OF GOD

Allow me to share a story with you that I told a local church a number of years ago. The story didn't go over too well. But I hope I can tell it in a way that you will understand and appreciate. You be the judge.

I was talking about worship and attempting to make the point that God loves to be worshiped because in worship we tell the truth about God. Here is how my speech went:

"Let's say that you walked up to your pastor and said to him, 'You know, you are the most perfect person in the world. I don't know of anyone any better than you. In you resides all truth, goodness, and beauty. You are good, you abound with compassion, you are holy and righteous, you are just and pure. I adore you and worship you. I extol you and praise your name.'

"What would your pastor do? Why, he would hang his head, wave you off and say, 'Don't say that, it embarrasses me.' Why would he respond that way? Because it's not true. [Here is where I got myself in trouble with the people. They all loved their pastor and would never say anything against him.]

"Suppose you speak words of worship and adoration to God. What would God do? Would God shuffle his feet in celestial dust, hang his head and say, Aw, shucks. No! Why not? Because for God—these words of worship are true!"

God loves to be worshiped. God loves to hear us say, "We worship and adore you, we bless you, for you and you alone are God. There is no one besides you." This is what we do in worship. We worship and adore God simply because of who God is.

Historically, the church has expressed its worship of God in the great act of praise called the Gloria in Excelsis Deo. This great hymn of praise extols God simply for who God is in God's character and being. It is a hymn of praise found in the "acts of entrance," through which God's people gather for worship.

> Glory to God in the highest,
> and peace to his people on earth.
> Lord God, heavenly King,
> almighty God and Father,
> we worship you,
> we give you thanks,
> we praise you for your glory.
> Lord Jesus Christ, only Son of the Father,
> Lord God, Lamb of God,
> you take away the sin of the world: have mercy on us;
> you are seated at the right hand of the Father: receive our prayer.
> For you alone are the Holy One,
> you alone are the Lord,
> you alone are the Most High,
> Jesus Christ,
> with the Holy Spirit,
> in the glory of God the Father. Amen.

WORSHIP REMEMBERS JESUS CHRIST

The God whom we worship doesn't simply sit in the heavens like some unmovable mover. The God whom we worship—the God of the Bible—is a God of action.

God acts in history. And the reason God acts in history is to save us, to rescue us, to free us, to liberate us.

Behind the theme of the God who rescues us is a story that we often tell in worship. Let me tell you a story as a way of getting at the story we tell in worship.

A few years ago a friend of mine, an Episcopal priest, said, "Bob, take me to an evangelical church. I've never been to one." So I did.

We went to a Sunday evening service at the Bible Church, a church not far from my home in Wheaton, Illinois. While we gathered and found our seats, the organist and pianist were playing warm, friendly, and inviting hymns and songs that were familiar to everyone.

Soon the song leader led us in enthusiastic congregational song as we sang some of the favorite gospel songs of the nineteenth and early twentieth centuries.

Then the associate pastor said, "Let us pray," and he prayed this prayer:

"Lord, we thank you that you created us in your image and that when we fell away from you, you did not leave us in our sin, but you came to us in the person of your son, who lived among us, was crucified for our sin, rose again to newness of life, and ascended into heaven. We now await his return to renew and re-create all things. Bless us as we worship in his home. Amen."

That's it, that's it, I said to myself. *That's what it's all about. We have come here to remember God's saving action in history: how God came to our rescue to free us and to liberate us from the power of evil.*

If you will look closely at your worship, you will see that this theme runs through all of public worship. It's in the hymns, the prayers, the Scripture readings, the sermon, the creed, and the prayers of thanksgiving over bread and wine.

Worship remembers the living, the dying, the rising of Christ. Through that action it promotes the overthrow of the powers of evil. How does the church in its worship remember this saving event? It tells the story at the service of the word. And it enacts the story at the service of the table. But more about this later.

WORSHIP IS AN EXPERIENCE OF THE HOLY SPIRIT

The most misunderstood and maligned member of the Godhead is the Holy Spirit. What role does the Holy Spirit play in worship?

- In worship we *adore and magnify* the Father.
- In worship we *remember* the work of the Son.
- In worship we *experience* the work of the Holy Spirit.

Most of us in the western world are better at adoring and remembering than we are at experiencing. But what does it mean to say that we experience the Holy Spirit?

The Holy Spirit has always been understood as the enabler. The Holy Spirit enables us to adore and magnify the Father. The Holy Spirit enables us to remember the work of the Son. And, as we are open to the enabling work of the Holy Spirit, the Holy Spirit brings us into communion with the Father and the Son.

Let me tell you a story.

Shortly after finishing my graduate education in theology, I went through a crisis of faith. In my formal education I had been taught an "evidence that demands a verdict" approach to the faith. But when I discovered that I could not prove God or find God in a textbook, or in a syllogism, my faith crashed.

It's a long story, but I ended up finding God, or, should I say, God ended up finding me in worship, especially at the Lord's table—at bread and wine.

In worship I experienced the Holy Spirit bringing the saving, healing, comforting, renewing power of God to me. As we open ourselves to the Holy Spirit working in worship, the Holy Spirit will enable us to experience the healing work of Christ and to know the reality of God. Faith is rekindled and revived—not by reasons that prove God—but by the enabling power of the Holy Spirit at work in worship.

WORSHIP IS THE SIGN OF THE FUTURE

Because I travel a lot, I'm a person who is very dependent on signs. When I leave an airport in a strange city to get to my destination, I'm always peering at the signs. When I see the sign that I'm looking for, the sign that says to me "go in this direction and you will get there," I feel a sense of relief come over me. I'm able to say "I'm on the way."

Signs are important. We all know that. But most Christians I know don't seem to be aware that worship is a sign of the future. What does this mean? Let me explain it this way.

Worship as a sign of the future is a momentary experience of the future. In worship we enter into the future, we experience the future, we stand in the future with the angels and archangels, with the cherubim and seraphim and with the whole company of saints in God's redeemed creation to cry and shout aloud, "Holy, Holy, Holy, the whole earth is full of your glory."

In this sense, worship anticipates the new heavens and the new earth—God's future for our history.

Worship Is My Response to God

Finally, we should note that there is a subjective side to worship. In worship we really do something. But what we do is always in response to what God is doing.

I have found a word in my own personal worship that best describes what we do in worship.

The word is "intention."

In worship we intend what it is that God would have in worship.

We intend to be open to God.

We intend to glorify and magnify God's name.

We intend to remember the living, the dying, and the rising of Christ, as well as the overthrow of the powers of evil.

We intend to receive the enabling power of the Holy Spirit.

We intend to be a sign of the church, the future of God's reign over the entire creation.

Conclusion

This study clearly shows us that worship has both a divine and a human side. The divine side is that God acts in worship to do for us what God has done for us throughout history. The human side is that we respond to God who is present in the acts of remembrance. In worship, divine action is continually met by human response—faith.

STUDY GUIDE

Read Session 2, "What Is Worship All About?"
before starting the study guide.

PART I: PERSONAL STUDY

Answer the following questions on your own.

1. *Life Connection*
♦ Do you remember the first time you became aware of worship renewal? Perhaps you heard a talk on the subject or someone mentioned a church in worship renewal. Describe that experience below.

_____

_____

_____

_____

_____

2. *Content Questions*
♦ Analyze the content of the Gloria in Excelsis Deo in the section "Worship Extols the Character of God." What does it say about God the Father, God the Son, God the Holy Spirit?

Father: _____

_____

Son: _____

_____

Holy Spirit: _____

_____

♦ Read Isaiah 6:1–7. What words does Isaiah use to magnify God?

_____

_____

_____

_____

_____

◆ Analyze the prayer prayed by the associate pastor in the section "Worship Remembers Jesus Christ." Draw a diagram or picture that captures the story line of this prayer.

◆ Read 1 Peter 2:9. How do the words "that you may proclaim the mighty acts of him who called you out of darkness into his marvelous light" relate to the story that worship celebrates? _____

_____

_____

_____

_____

_____

◆ In the section "Worship Is an Experience of the Holy Spirit," we described the Holy Spirit as the one who enables worship. Describe what the Holy Spirit does in worship. _____

_____

_____

_____

_____

_____

◆ Read John 16:12–15. How does this passage relate the Holy Spirit to worship? _____

_____

_____

_____

_____

_____

◆ Explain what it means to say that worship is a "sign of the future."

_____
_____
_____
_____
_____
_____

◆ Read Acts 2:42–47. How is worship a "sign of the future" in Jerusalem in A.D. 30? _____

_____
_____
_____
_____
_____

◆ The previous questions looked at worship from an objective point of view. Now we will look at the subjective side. How do you answer this question, What do we do in worship?_____

_____
_____
_____
_____
_____

3. *Application*

◆ Before you answer the following questions, obtain a bulletin or an order of worship from a recent service in your church.

◆ Study the bulletin of your worship and find all the hymns, prayers, and expressions of worship that express adoration to God.

◆ Where in your worship would you add additional expressions of adoration to God? _____

_____
_____
_____

◆ Study the worship of your church to find the ways in which it "tells the story" of God's salvation. Describe how it does this below:

_____

_____

_____

_____

_____

◆ How would you improve the "story line" in the worship of your church?

_____

_____

_____

_____

_____

◆ How would you describe the presence and activity of the Holy Spirit in your worship? _____

_____

_____

_____

_____

_____

◆ How may the experience of the presence of the Holy Spirit be improved in the worship of your church? _____

_____

_____

_____

_____

_____

◆ How do you experience worship as a sign of the future in your church worship? _____

_____

_____

_____

- How may worship as the sign of the future be improved in the worship of your church? _____

_____

_____

_____

_____

- How would you help and encourage personal intention in the worship of your church? _____

_____

_____

_____

_____

PART II: GROUP DISCUSSION

Write all of the group members' answers to the questions in each section on a chalkboard or flip chart.

1. *Life Connection*
- Begin the group session by asking several members to recite their experience of first hearing about or first experiencing worship renewal.

2. *Thought Questions*
- Read Isaiah 6:1–7 and comment on how Isaiah meets God in God's transcendence. Next, explore how the worship of your church extols the character of God. Ask for examples from hymns and prayers in the worship of your church.
- Read 1 Peter 2:9 and comment on the meaning of the phrase "that you may proclaim the mighty acts of him who called you out of darkness into his marvelous light." Explore how the worship of your church remembers the mighty deeds of salvation.

- Read John 16:12–25 and comment on how this passage relates to the work of the Holy Spirit in worship. Explore the experience of the Holy Spirit in your worship.

- Read Acts 2:42–47 and comment on how the church prefigures relationships in the new heavens and the new earth. Explore how the worship of your church is an expression of the future.

- Explore the kind of intention you bring to worship. How does each person in the group prepare for worship?

3. *Application*

- How can the act of extolling God be improved in the worship of your church?

- How can the act of remembering God's mighty deeds of salvation be improved in the worship of your church?

- How can the experience of the Holy Spirit be intensified in the worship of your church?

- How can the experience of the church as an expression of the future kingdom be made more real?

- How would you go about helping people to intensify their intentionality in worship?

DOES WORSHIP HAVE A STRUCTURE?

A Study in the Order of Worship

As far back as I can remember, I was always told that my life had to be organized by some kind of structure that gave it meaning: "this is the time you get up, this is the time you eat, this is the time you go to bed." I wasn't always happy about the structure, feeling sometimes that it was imposed upon me. But when I got up too early, went without a meal, or went to bed too late, I understood the wisdom of structure.

In spite of the commonsense wisdom of structure, I derived the conviction somewhere and from someone that worship was not subject to the laws of structure (even though worship was structured in our free church, in fact, structured the same way every Sunday). Worship, I was taught, was to be free, spontaneous, and unstructured.

Now, in the later years of my life, I know that all of life is structured and interconnected, and follows certain patterns—including worship.

As I have thought about the structure and pattern of worship, I have seen an analogy to what we do when we invite guests over for dinner. Let me explain the analogy.

LET'S MEET FOR DINNER

Let's imagine for a moment that you and I are good friends. We have spent a great deal of time together, growing fond of each other and enjoying each other's company. So I invite you to come over for dinner after church. Let's see how this meeting over food is structured.

I'm in my house preparing the meal and looking forward to your arrival. As soon as you knock on the door, I run to the door with great anticipation, swing the door open wide, smile warmly, and say, "Welcome! Come in, so good to see you. Let me have your coat." I may shake your hand or embrace you and say other words of greeting that express my happiness at seeing you.

Then I invite you into the family room and bid you to relax and make yourself feel at home. I bring you something to drink and put a plate of hors d'oeuvres on the coffee table. We nibble at the food, sip our drink, and talk enthusiastically to each other about things that matter as we connect and communicate.

Then dinner is ready. My wife, who has been making the final preparations, says "Okay, we're ready. Come, gather around the table. Let's eat." We all sit and I say, "Let's pray." We grasp each other's hands, bow our heads, and pray. And then we eat. And as we eat, we talk to each other in an animated and joyous way. We enjoy the food. We enjoy each other's company, and we communicate as we eat our salad and main course, and finish with pie and coffee. We sit back in our chairs, relax, and talk on of things that we hold in common, things that interest us, things about which we are passionate.

Finally, you say, "It's getting late, and I've got to be going home." We then shift into another mood and mode—the thank-you, farewell, and come-again rituals. I walk you to the door. I shake your hand or embrace you again, telling you how good it was to be together with you. I assure you that we must do this again. It was enjoyable and enriching to be together. So off you go, happy to have been with me, feeling good about the afternoon, about yourself, and about our relationship.

Let's stop for a moment and reflect on what was going on here. It was a meeting: a gathering of people who talked, ate, and fellowshiped together. Communication was going on. Relationship was happening. Community was being formed.

But note that all of this occurred in the context of a structure that we all have played out a hundred times over. It was a structure, actually a ritual, of communication that was characterized by four parts—acts of entrance, a ritual of communication, a ritual of eating, and acts of dismissal. Each of these acts and rituals occurred with an obvious flow, a discernible movement that transmitted a progressive development of relationship. It would be unthinkable to mix these acts up, put them out of sequence, or reverse them. Such a rearrangement would disorder the entire meaning of a dinner relationship.

When we gather together to worship, we follow a similar sequence. We meet with God at God's house where we enter, communicate, eat at God's table, and go forth into the world.

Meet Me at the Mountain

In the Old Testament the mountain was a place of meeting between God and Israel. At Mount Sinai God delivered the Ten Commandments through Moses and there, at the mountain, the people entered into covenant with God. This meeting, the first act of public worship recorded in Scripture, is described in Exodus 24:1–8.

Then he [the LORD] said to Moses, "Come up to the LORD, you and Aaron, Nadab and Abihu, and seventy of the elders of Israel. You are to worship at a distance, but Moses alone is to approach the LORD; the others must not come near. And the people may not come up with him." When Moses went and told the people all the LORD's words and laws, they responded with one voice, "Everything the LORD has said we will do." Moses then wrote down everything the LORD had said. He got up early the next morning and built an altar at the foot of the mountain and set up twelve stone pillars representing the twelve tribes of Israel. Then he sent young Israelite men, and they offered burnt offerings and sacrificed young bulls as fellowship offerings to the LORD. Moses took half of the blood and put it in bowls, and the other half he sprinkled on the altar. Then he took the Book of the Covenant and read it to the people. They responded, "We will do everything the LORD has said; we will obey." Moses then took the blood, sprinkled it on the people and said, "This is the blood of the covenant that the LORD has made with you in accordance with all these words."

A close study of this meeting at the mountain shows that it includes all the structural elements of worship—acts of entrance, communication of the word, a covenant meal, and a sending forth with a purpose.

GATHER TO HEAR THE STORY, BREAK THE BREAD, AND GO FORTH TO SERVE

Once Andrew Greeley was being interviewed on the radio about his books and other matters, including his work as a Catholic priest. One of the callers who was curious about worship asked, "Father Greeley, what do you do when you worship?" His answer was simple and to the point and directly related to the subject of this chapter. "Well," he said, "we gather the people, tell the story, break bread, and go home."

His answer was simple but very biblical and very profound.

The earliest description of Christian worship is given in Acts 2:42. Think about this description of worship in Jerusalem and reflect on its structure. "They devoted themselves to the apostles' teaching and to the fellowship, to the breaking of the bread and to prayer."

The two central foci of early Christian worship were the apostolic teaching (the story) and the breaking of the bread (the feast). And these two acts were performed as prayer and in the context of fellowship.

Later, as descriptions of Christian worship began to emerge, the church paid attention to how people gathered and how people were sent forth.

CONCLUSION

We have been exploring the structure of worship in this session.

How should worship be ordered? The biblical insight on this question is not complex. It is as simple as inviting guests into your home.

As you gather to worship or as you plan worship, keep this simple structure in mind. As you would carefully think through how to entertain someone in your home, informally or formally—so think through how you want to conduct these four parts of a relationship with God in the house where you worship.

STUDY GUIDE

Read Session 3, "Does Worship Have a Structure?"
before starting the study guide.

PART I: PERSONAL STUDY

Answer the following questions on your own.

1. *Life Connection*

• Most people follow a deliberate structure or pattern throughout a typical day. In the space below, outline your daily structure from the time you get up to the time you go to bed. What kind of structure or pattern emerges? How do you respond to interruptions to your daily schedule?

_____

_____

_____

_____

• How do you feel about the structure or order of worship? Do you like it to be (1) the same, (2) similar, or (3) filled with variety?

2. *Content Questions*

• In the text a comparison was made between the structure of worship and entertaining someone for dinner in your home. Respond to this analogy. What new insights did you gain from it? _____

_____

_____

_____

_____

• Read and study Exodus 24:1–8. Find the following elements of worship in this text and write them down.

Acts of entrance _____

_____

Communication of the word _____

_____

A covenant meal (act of sacrifice) _____

_____

A sending forth (implied) _____

_____

◆ Study Acts 2:42. What are the two central foci of early Christian worship?

_____

_____

_____

_____

3. *Application*

◆ In the space below, write out the order of your worship (you may need a bulletin). _____

_____

_____

_____

_____

_____

◆ Identify the acts of entrance. _____

_____

_____

_____

◆ Identify the elements of worship that fulfill the apostolic teaching (story).

_____

_____

_____

◆ Identify the acts of worship that fulfill the breaking of the bread (feast).

_____

_____

_____

- Identify the acts of worship that fulfill the sending forth.

  _____

  _____

  _____

- What is God doing in each of these four parts of worship?

  _____

  _____

  _____

  _____

  _____

- What happens in the people's hearts during each of these four parts of worship? _____

  _____

  _____

  _____

  _____

- In what ways is the worship of your church analogous to the relationships that happen in your home when you entertain guests? _____

  _____

  _____

  _____

  _____

PART II: GROUP DISCUSSION

Write all of the group members' answers to the questions in each section on a chalkboard or flip chart.

1. *Life Connection*
- Ask several people to summarize their daily schedules. Then pose this question: Should worship have a structure?

2. *Thought Questions*

♦ Ask the group to comment on the analogy between the structure of worship and entertaining friends in the home. Do they see the connections?

♦ Compare notes on Exodus 24:1–8. Did people find the four parts of worship in this example?

♦ Read Acts 2:42. Does the group agree on the two central foci of worship as story and feast?

3. *Application*

♦ Write the order of worship from a recent service on the board or flip chart. Then analyze and discuss the service.

♦ Identify:

the acts of entrance

the apostolic teaching (story)

the breaking of the bread (feast)

the sending forth

♦ Ask:

What do you sense God is doing in these parts of worship? Take time to deal with each part.

What do you do in each phase of worship that is directed toward God?

What happens in your heart and life in each phase of worship?

How can our worship be strengthened on both the vertical plane and the horizontal plane?

IS THERE ONLY ONE STYLE
OF WORSHIP?

A Study in the Variety of Worship Styles

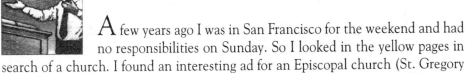 A few years ago I was in San Francisco for the weekend and had no responsibilities on Sunday. So I looked in the yellow pages in search of a church. I found an interesting ad for an Episcopal church (St. Gregory Nyssen Episcopal Church) that said something like "we worship according to an early church style with congregational participation and strong use of the arts." I said to myself, "That's it! That's where I'll go."

The worship of this church followed the fourfold sequence discussed in session 3, but with a flair that made it quite different from any other Episcopal church I have attended.

We used two different spaces—one for the service of the word and another for the service of the table. Each space stood at the opposite end of a large and open square room. At one end was a huge round table and at the other end were chairs facing each other flanked on one end by a pulpit (with an African liturgical flag and a Tibetan gong). On the other end was a simple platform with three chairs in the midst of liturgical flags and banners. We moved from one space to the other singing hymns and dancing to the rhythm of the music.

The service of the word was quite participatory. We sang not only hymns but also choruses and alleluias of the African tradition. The people were all involved in the prayers.

The people also responded to the sermon by standing to make a comment, give a word of testimony, or deliver an exhortation.

After the service of the word, we danced back to the table, the Eucharistic space, where we formed a community around the table, passed the kiss of peace, received the bread and wine, and then danced around the table as we sang. This was followed by an enjoyable agape feast of fruit, breads, and nuts.

About a year later I was invited to speak at a worship conference at Christ's Church in Nashville, a large Pentecostal church. I wasn't prepared for what I was about to experience.

I have an image about how Pentecostal worship is supposed to be, even as I have an image about how Episcopal worship is usually expressed. My experience of worship at Christ's Church took me by surprise, just as the service at St. Gregory Nyssen Church had done.

Christ's Church is a large church set on a hill among some of the most beautiful trees you have ever seen. The church has grown rather rapidly and it consists of a church building within a church building. The older, smaller structure and sanctuary for worship was intentionally contained within the architecture of the new building.

Every Sunday morning, during the Sunday school hour, this Pentecostal church celebrates a Eucharist (yes, they use the word "Eucharist") in the old sanctuary. I was told, "Be sure you go to the Sunday morning Eucharist."

I arrived a bit early and there were a few people milling around, so I took a seat in the front row and waited in a spirit of quietness and prayer.

As I was sitting there, a few thoughts ran through my mind. "A Eucharist in a Pentecostal church. I wonder what they will do?" Since there were only a few people in the sanctuary, I expected that a total of twenty-five to fifty people would eventually come.

To my surprise, the entire sanctuary filled up by the time the singing started. I would guess that nearly five hundred people attended this Eucharist.

As we sang, the minister processed to his place—nothing unusual about that except he was wearing a robe and carrying the *Book of Common Prayer*, the prayer book of the Episcopal Church! My interest and curiosity were raised several notches, believe me.

The service progressed through the four acts—entrance, word, table, and dismissal—following the ancient structure that you will find in liturgical churches all over the world. But the service was conducted with a *decided* Pentecostal flavor. It was characterized by Pentecostal music, Pentecostal prayer circles, the raising of hands, speaking in tongues, an anointing of oil for the sick, and plenty of strong, heartfelt, Pentecostal enthusiasm in a highly participatory service.

Now we have to ask ourselves, What's going on here? When did the Episcopal liturgy change and become so thoroughly participatory? How is it that a Pentecostal church follows the fourfold pattern of the ancient church and uses some of the prayers from the *Book of Common Prayer*?

I think the best way to explain this phenomenon is as a convergence of worship, a blending of the traditional with the contemporary. For our purposes, it demonstrates that there is no such thing as one style.

The content of worship, which is the story of God's redeeming work in Jesus Christ, is absolutely nonnegotiable. The structure of worship—which proclaims and enacts the story and thus creates a meeting between God and God's people in which a relationship is established, maintained, and repaired—is rooted in Scripture and common experience. But the style of worship—traditional, contemporary, convergence, Black, Spanish, or some other style—is totally dependent on the cultural heritage and preference of the worshiping community.

STYLE IN THE NEW TESTAMENT

This rich variety of style is rooted in the New Testament itself, where we find at least three descriptions of worship, each of which expresses a different style. Let's take a look at the New Testament record.

First, there is the house church style. Read Acts 2:42–47 to get a good strong feeling for this worship. Here, for example, are some of the elements of worship that were included as these people went from house to house worshiping God:

- Apostolic teaching
- Breaking of bread (agape feast)
- Prayer
- Fellowship
- Signs and wonders
- Community
- Praise
- Joy
- Growth

Today there are many churches that seek to continue this primitive model of worship, particularly the Mennonite and Brethren communities, who opt for biblical simplicity in worship as well as lifestyle.

Second, we are able to identify a worship in the Corinthian church that may be best described as body life worship. This worship is presented in 1 Corinthians 12–14. However, it is important to note that this letter to the Corinthians alludes to many aspects of worship. Read chapter 12, for example, to get the flavor of body life. Here is a sample from that passage:

> Now you are the body of Christ, and each one of you is a part of it. And in the church God has appointed first of all apostles, second prophets, third teachers, then workers of miracles, also those having gifts of healing, those able to help others, those with gifts of administration, and those

speaking in different kinds of tongues. Are all apostles? Are all prophets? Are all teachers? Do all work miracles? Do all have gifts of healing? Do all speak in tongues? Do all interpret? (1 Cor 12:27–30)

We can readily see from this passage of Scripture that the worship of the church is one—each person bringing a particular gift to worship and exercising that gift within the body.

Today, the phenomena known as the charismatic movement—a movement of the Spirit that is found in nearly all the denominations of the world—expresses best the style of Corinthian worship. Some people strongly oppose this movement because of its enthusiasm. While some in the movement may show excessive enthusiasm, we all need to recognize that it is rooted in the experience of the first-century church.

Third, there is liturgical worship in the New Testament. Liturgical worship is found throughout the book of Revelation, but it is best described in chapters 4–5. Read these passages and note the stunning setting, the beauty of space, the glorious heavenly language, the antiphonal singing, the incense and the prayers. Here, for example, is a brief excerpt from that marvelous description of liturgical worship.

Whenever the living creatures give glory, honor and thanks to him who sits on the throne and lives for ever and ever, the twenty-four elders fall down before him who sits on the throne, and worship him who lives for ever and ever. They lay their crowns before the throne and say: "You are worthy, our Lord and God, to receive glory and honor and power, for you created all things, and by your will they were created and have their being." (Rev 4:9–11)

Today many, perhaps most, of the world's churches are liturgical. The Orthodox and Roman Catholic communities worship according to liturgical style, as do the Anglicans, the Episcopalians, the Lutherans, and many mainline denominations that are moving toward a worship that is more liturgical.

STYLES OF WORSHIP TODAY

Throughout the history of the church the styles of worship have not changed significantly. We can point to the long and enduring history of liturgical worship, or we can identify the history of traditional Protestant worship coming from Reformation times, or we can look at the free church worship of the modern era in the churches that are neither historic nor traceable to the sixteenth-century Reformation.

However, the latter part of the twentieth century has produced a revolution in worship, introducing a variety of new styles that have shaken the churches of the world. In part 3 of this study we will look more closely at these old and new forms of worship that are raising so many questions about style.

CONCLUSION

What are we to make of the many styles of worship? Some people want to make an issue of style, when it should *not* be an issue.

The content of worship is the gospel story and is nonnegotiable; the structure has roots in biblical and historical tradition, as well as the common experience of the people, and is therefore natural to all. But style is individual, tied into the particular history, culture, and personal preferences of a particular people.

Consequently, style is not an issue to fight and divide over, but something to discuss on the level of personal preference.

STUDY GUIDE

Read Session 4, "Is There Only One Style of Worship?"
before starting the study guide.

PART I: PERSONAL STUDY

Answer the following questions on your own.

1. *Life Connection*

◆ Recall one or two unusual worship experiences you have had. What made them so different, so unique? Use the space below for your remembrances. _____

_____

_____

_____

_____

_____

_____

◆ How do you feel about blended worship, in which the worship of your church draws from other traditions of worship?

❑ I am strongly in favor of blended worship.
❑ I am mildly in favor of blended worship.
❑ I am neutral toward blended worship.
❑ I am mildly against blended worship.
❑ I am strongly against blended worship.
❑ I am not really certain what blended worship would be like at my church.

2. *Content Questions*

◆ House church worship is described in Acts 2:42–47. On the following list, check whether those elements of house church worship are found in your church. Then use the blank provided to the right of each expression of worship to indicate how each aspect that you checked as "yes" is expressed in the worship of your church.

```
Yes  No
 ❏   ❏   Apostolic teaching _____
 ❏   ❏   Breaking of bread _____
 ❏   ❏   Prayer _____
 ❏   ❏   Fellowship _____
 ❏   ❏   Signs and wonders_____
 ❏   ❏   Community _____
 ❏   ❏   Praise _____
 ❏   ❏   Joy _____
 ❏   ❏   Growth _____
```

◆ Body life worship is described in 1 Corinthians 12–14. Read and analyze 1 Corinthians 12:27–31. Then list the specific gifts on the left. On the right, describe how this gift is expressed in the worship of your church.

Gift   Expression of Gift

_____   _____

_____   _____

_____   _____

_____   _____

_____   _____

_____   _____

_____   _____

_____   _____

◆ Liturgical worship is described in Revelation 4 and 5. In the space below, capture the spatial and visual description of chapter 4 in a drawing. If you don't like to draw, simply list the words that express the beauty of the worship described.

◆ In your own words, summarize the distinction between content, structure, and style.

Content _____

Structure _____

Style _____

3. *Application*

◆ Check the type of worship that is closest to the worship practiced in your church.

   ❑ House church worship

   ❑ Body life worship

   ❑ Liturgical worship

◆ What would you like your church to borrow from house church worship?

_____

_____

_____

_____

◆ What would you like your church to borrow from body life worship?

_____

_____

_____

_____

◆ What would you like your church to borrow from liturgical worship?

_____

_____

_____

_____

◆ Do you feel that one of these worship styles best expresses your praise and thanks to God? If so, which style and why?

_____

_____

_____

_____

PART II: GROUP DISCUSSION

Write all of the group members' answers to the questions in each section on a chalkboard or flip chart.

1. *Life Connection*

◆ Begin by asking several members of the group to tell a story of an unusual worship experience.

◆ Poll the group to find out how many are in favor (strongly, mildly) of blended worship; how many are against (strongly, mildly) blended worship; how many are neutral; and how many are not certain what blended worship is all about.

2. *Thought Questions*

◆ Read Acts 2:42–47. Ask, "How does our worship compare with the worship of the house church?" Keep the focus of the discussion on comparison, and hold application questions.

◆ Read 1 Corinthians 12:1–31. Ask, "How does our worship compare with the body life worship of the Corinthian church?" Keep the focus of the discussion on comparison, and hold application questions.

◆ Read Revelation 4:1–11. Ask, "How does our worship compare with the liturgical worship of the early church?" Keep the focus of the discussion on comparison, and hold application questions.

3. *Application*

◆ What could your church borrow from the house church tradition of worship?

◆ What could your church borrow from the body life tradition of worship?

◆ What could your church borrow from the liturgical tradition of worship?

◆ In which style of worship can you offer your praise to God best? Why?

PART II

WHAT DOES
WORSHIP DO?

WORSHIP GATHERS THE PEOPLE

A Study in the Acts of Entrance

 For the past several summers I've had the opportunity to experience a number of weddings, including one in my own family. I suppose it's because my children and their friends are at that marrying age and because so many of my personal friends are at the age when their children are walking down the aisle.

I never attend a wedding without experiencing the feeling of joy and excitement that surrounds the ringing of those bells. As I reflect on the weddings I've attended, I'm becoming increasingly aware of the entrance rituals that establish the spirit of joy and excitement.

I usually arrive a little early and make my way to the foyer of the church to greet the family and friends of the wedding party. These greetings mostly consist of handshakes, hugs, and small talk. The small talk is always of the cheery kind with the usual remarks, for example, "You look really good; that dress looks beautiful on you; the church really looks nice; congratulations on your new daughter-in-law; they really are a handsome couple," and so on.

Then I find my seat, listen quietly to the music, and wait for the procession.

I've always had this special relationship with a procession. There is something about the decorated church, the energy of the congregation, the wedding march, and the dramatic appearance of the bride and her father that grabs me in the stomach and touches the emotional side of my person.

What I have briefly described here are opening rituals. These movements of word and touch are important because they set the stage for what is to follow. Furthermore, these are common rituals. Whether you are Orthodox, Catholic, mainline Protestant, evangelical, Pentecostal, or charismatic, you go through these rituals at a wedding. They start the movement, they signal the beginning, they provide the necessary flow into the ceremony of marriage where vows and rings and kisses are exchanged to seal before public witnesses the mystery we call marriage.

Let's apply all this to what we do in worship.

WHAT DOES AN ENTRANCE DO?

In a wedding, two people come together to get married. The importance and significance of this event are expressed in the rituals of entrance. These rituals are not the wedding itself, but they are important actions that deliver the participants to the event—the exchange of vows and rings.

Worship, like a wedding, is an event. In this event, we once again tell the story of the meaning of life. We speak of the conflict between good and evil and proclaim Christ as the victor over all evil in this world and in our life now. The heart of worship is to remember God's saving deeds and to anticipate the new heavens and the new earth. As we *remember* and *anticipate*, our covenantal relationship with God is renewed. We are empowered to live in God's name in a way that is victorious over the powers of evil, so they cannot tempt us away from our relationship with God.

Because this event of worship is so central and so important to our lives, the *gathering acts* of worship, which bring us to the remembrance of God's saving deeds and to an anticipation of the future, take on a special significance. The gathering acts are a kind of spiritual journey through which people travel.

Let me give you an example.

In second-century worship there were no significant acts of entrance to worship. People would gather in the house where they were to worship and greet each other with words of welcome and conversation. After all had gathered, the minister would simply say, "The Lord be with you" to which all the people would respond "And with your spirit." The people then took their seats and the service of the Word began with the reading of Scripture.

By the fourth century, when the church had become large and met in basilicas, the church recognized the need for acts of entrance that gathered the people in a more significant and dramatic way. The greater size of the community no longer fit the more casual entrance of the second-century house church.

The biblical clue for the acts of entrance came from the Old Testament example of the gathering for the dedication of the temple found in 2 Chronicles 5:11–14. Here we see the importance of the *approach* to God and an example of how a large crowd of worshipers came together and assembled for worship.

All the Levites who were musicians—Asaph, Heman, Jeduthun and their sons and relatives— stood on the east side of the altar, dressed in fine linen and playing cymbals, harps and lyres. They were accompanied by 120 priests sounding trumpets. The trumpeters and singers joined in unison, as with one voice, to give praise and thanks to the LORD. Accompanied by trumpets, cymbals and other instruments, they raised their voices in praise to the LORD and sang, "He is good; his love endures forever." Then the temple of the LORD was filled with a cloud, and the priests could not perform their service because of the cloud, for the glory of the LORD filled the temple of God. (2 Chron 5:12–14)

So, what does an entrance do? An entrance is comprised of acts of worship that bring people into the presence of God and prepare them to hear the word of the Lord. Let me give you three examples—a traditional, a contemporary, and a convergence entrance.

ACTS OF ENTRANCE IN TRADITIONAL WORSHIP

Traditional worship attempts to accomplish the goal of bringing the congregation to the Word through the following acts:

- Prelude
- Entrance hymn
- Greeting
- Call to worship
- Invocation
- Act of praise
- Confession and forgiveness
- Opening prayer

The purpose of the prelude is to give the congregation a time for silent preparation, whereas the entrance hymn begins the formal act of public worship. In liturgical churches, the entrance hymn is accompanied by a procession of ministers and choir with crosses, banners, and incense that express the great joy of traveling into a meeting with God.

When the worship leaders have taken their places, a greeting, a call to worship, and an invocation are formal signs that the meeting with God has begun. The meeting takes on a more intense expression as the congregation sings an act of praise (most often the Gloria in Excelsis Deo), which extols God and magnifies God's name. The congregation, now in the very presence of God, the transcendent and Holy One, confesses its sin (as in Isaiah 6) and then hears the comforting words of God's forgiveness and acceptance.

Finally, an opening prayer brings closure to the acts of entrance and opens the way to the service of the word, where the people will hear and respond to God, who becomes present through his word.

ACTS OF ENTRANCE IN CONTEMPORARY WORSHIP

Contemporary worship is strikingly different from traditional worship, yet it seeks to do the very same thing traditional worship seeks to do, which is to ready the people to hear the word of the Lord. One of several models of contemporary worship follows the Old Testament tabernacle model and leads people through the gates and ultimately into the holy of holies. For example, the shape of the acts of entrance in a contemporary worship setting may look like this:

- ◆ Entrance through the gates
- ◆ Praise in the outer and inner courts
- ◆ Worship in the holy of holies

This sequence or journey toward the word is usually accomplished through praise and worship songs interlaced with appropriate admonitions from Scripture.

For example, the congregation may begin with a song or songs that express the act of going through gates. One popular song that expresses this idea is Leona Von Brethorst's "He Has Made Me Glad (I Will Enter His Gates)," which contains the lyrics, "I will enter His gates with thanksgiving in my heart, I will enter His courts with praise."

Once in the outer court, the congregation sings songs about coming to worship, such as "I Will Call upon the Lord," by Michael O'Shields, and "Come and Worship," by Don Moen. These songs are usually robust and loud, accompanied by shouts and dancing. But once the worship leader admonishes the people to enter into the inner court, the mood becomes more quiet. Here the congregation sings songs about God such as "You are the Mighty King," by Eddie Espinosa, or "We Will Glorify," by Twila Paris. Finally, the congregation becomes very quiet as the movement is made into the holy of holies. Now the people may assume a posture of humble kneeling, and perhaps some of the worshipers will be prostrate on the floor as songs are sung to God, such as "I Love You, Lord," by Laurie Klein, or "Father, I Adore You," by Terrye Coelho. These acts of entrance may be closed with a prayer.

ACTS OF ENTRANCE IN CONVERGENCE WORSHIP

A third approach to the acts of entrance, which is coming into use in churches all over the world, is the convergence of the traditional and contemporary. Attraction to convergence worship is prompted by the Holy Spirit as congregations realize the spiritual value of both the traditional and the contemporary. The historic approach is characterized by the sense of being rooted in the church's tradition, while the contemporary approach is characterized by the sense of the Spirit's immediacy.

No single acceptable universal pattern of a convergence worship entrance has emerged, but here is a possible order:

- Gathering songs
- Entrance hymn with procession
- Greeting, call to worship, and invocation
- Songs of praise and worship
- Confession
- Opening prayer

The gathering songs, which take the place of the prelude, are sung as the people find their seats. These songs may bring the people through the gates and into the outer court, where songs of coming to worship are sung. Then, the entrance hymn (a classic hymn, not a chorus or gospel song) signals the movement into the inner court, where the greeting, call to worship, and invocation occur. Finally, a variety of songs of praise and worship, ranging from ancient to modern, may be sung, followed by a time of confession as the worshipers stand in the manifest presence of God. And again, closure to the acts of entrance and openness to the word occur in the opening prayer.

HOW IS THE JOURNEY OF ENTRANCE CHANGING?

The three examples I have given you above show that the spiritual journey of the entrance is changing. It may be changing in your own church. So let's summarize how these acts of opening worship are being reshaped in many churches.

First, and possibly foremost, it is important to recognize that the acts of entrance are changing from program to narrative. A program is a series of unrelated and unconnected acts strung together without a sense of moving the congregation from one place to another. For example, a worship committee may say, "Let's see, we need a hymn, a Scripture, a prayer, and maybe something else to fit in between." This kind of thinking does not allow for movement, for journey, for narrative. A narrative, on the other hand, moves the people sequentially as in the liturgical tradition, from a processional hymn to a call to worship, to an invocation, an act of praise, and an opening prayer. The content of each of these acts of worship moves or "narrates" the people into the presence of God.

A second significant change taking place in worship today is the focus on music. The best example of this change is seen in contemporary worship.

The acts of entrance are carried out almost exclusively in song with a few appropriate comments here and there. In addition, a wide variety of musical instruments has come to be utilized, including the guitar, the drums, and the synthesizer. While these instruments are used primarily in contemporary worshiping communities, their use in traditional churches is growing too.

A third change is in the increased use of the arts, particularly in the procession. While processions bespeak movement into the presence of God and have been used historically in liturgical churches, they are now being used in many contemporary churches. These processions use banners and dance in new and creative ways.

Finally, it is important to recognize that the acts of entrance are becoming longer. In traditional churches, the acts of entrance take less than ten minutes, but in contemporary churches the acts of entrance (often called worship time) are generally thirty minutes in length. Convergence churches will spend anywhere from fifteen to thirty minutes in the entrance, depending on the length of the service (many churches have lengthened the service to an hour and a half).

Conclusion

Worship, as we have seen, begins by gathering the people. The ritual of gathering is important because it establishes a tone of warmth and joy, it narrates the people into the presence of God, and it readies them to hear the word of the Lord. It is a spiritual journey into the presence of God, a journey toward the word where God speaks a decisive word into our lives.

Read Session 5, "Worship Gathers the People,"
before starting the study guide.

PART I: PERSONAL STUDY

Answer the following questions on your own.

1. *Life Connection*

◆ Think about the acts of entrance at a recent wedding or some other important event. Try to remember the details of gathering the people and preparing them for the event. Record that event and its detail below.

_____

_____

_____

_____

_____

◆ Recall a significant worship or religious event you recently attended. How were the people gathered for this event?

_____

_____

_____

_____

◆ In what sense is the gathering of the people for worship a spiritual journey?

_____

_____

_____

_____

_____

2. *Content Questions*

♦ Explain how worship is an event. What are we doing in worship that gives it an event character? _____

_____

_____

_____

♦ Why have the entrance acts of worship taken on such significance?

_____

_____

_____

_____

♦ Describe the acts of entrance in a second-century house church setting.

_____

_____

_____

_____

♦ Why did the fourth-century church begin to pay more attention to the acts of entrance? _____

_____

_____

_____

_____

♦ Read 2 Chronicles 5:11–14. Draw a picture of the act of gathering the people for the dedication of the temple or describe it in your own words.

♦ How would you explain the *spiritual journey* depicted in 2 Chronicles 5:11–14? _____

_____

_____

_____

♦ Explain each of the following acts of entrance in the traditional church. What does each act do in the spiritual journey taking place in the entrance?

Prelude_____

_____

Entrance hymn _____

_____

Greeting_____

_____

Call to worship _____

_____

Invocation _____

_____

Act of praise _____

_____

Confession and forgiveness_____

_____

Opening prayer _____

_____

♦ Explain each of the following acts of entrance in a contemporary church and describe the spiritual journey through which the people travel.

Entrance through the gates_____

_____

Praise in the outer court _____

_____

Praise in the inner court _____

_____

Worship in the holy of holies_____

_____

◆ Explain each of the following acts of entrance in a worship that blends the traditional and the contemporary. Describe the spiritual journey through which the people travel.

Gathering songs _____

_____

Entrance hymn with procession _____

_____

Greeting _____

_____

Call to worship _____

_____

Invocation _____

_____

Songs of praise and worship _____

_____

Confession _____

_____

Opening prayer _____

_____

◆ List the four ways in which the acts of worship are changing today, and comment on each.

a. _____

_____

_____

b. _____

_____

_____

c. _____

_____

_____

d. _____

_____

_____

3. *Application*

♦ Of the three types of entrance, which best describes the practice in your church?

❑ Traditional   ❑ Contemporary   ❑ Blended

♦ On the lines below list the acts of entrance in your church and for each act comment on the spiritual journey through which the people travel.

_____

_____

_____

_____

_____

_____

_____

_____

_____

_____

_____

_____

_____

♦ What would you like to see your church *borrow* from each style of entrance studied in this session?

Traditional _____

_____

Contemporary _____

_____

Blended _____

_____

♦ In the space provided prepare a proposed order for the acts of entrance. On the right, explain what each act of worship will do to gather the people and ready them to hear the word of the Lord. Remember to emphasize the narrative of coming together rather than creating a program. What you want to do is bring the people through a spiritual journey.

Proposed order   *What each act accomplishes*

_____   _____

_____   _____

_____   _____

_____   _____

_____   _____

_____   _____

_____   _____

PART II: GROUP DISCUSSION

Write all of the group members' answers to the questions in each section on a chalkboard or flip chart.

1. *Life Connection*

♦ Begin the group study by asking several people to comment on the gathering acts of a recent wedding or other important event.

♦ Ask the group to compare their experience of the gathering at the event described above with a recent gathering for worship.

2. *Thought Questions*

♦ Describe what it means to say that worship is an event.

♦ What do you think it means to say that the acts of entrance are a spiritual journey?

♦ Why would the acts of entrance in a house church different from the acts of entrance in a basilica?

♦ Read 2 Chronicles 5:11–14. Describe what is happening to the people spiritually as they make their entrance into the temple.

♦ Put the acts of entrance in a traditional church on the chalkboard or flip chart. Explain the spiritual significance of each act by asking, (1) What is God doing in this act? (2) What are the people experiencing in this act?

- Put the acts of entrance in a contemporary church on the chalkboard or flip chart. Explain the spiritual significance of each act by asking: (1) What is God doing in this act? (2) What are the people experiencing in this act?
- Put the acts of entrance in a blended church on the chalkboard or flip chart. Explain the spiritual significance of each act by asking: (1) What is God doing in this act? (2) What are the people experiencing in this act?
- How have the acts of entrance changed in your church recently?

3. *Application*

- List the acts of entrance from a recent bulletin of your church on the chalkboard or flip chart. Analyze these acts by answering the following questions.
- What do you sense God doing through these acts of entrance?
- Describe your experience in these acts of entrance.
- Would you describe these acts of entrance as a program or a narrative? Explain.
- What would you include from traditional worship?
- What would you include from contemporary worship?
- Ask for several members of the group to present their proposed order for the acts of entrance that they have prepared. As you discuss each of the proposed orders, do so by following the questions above.

WORSHIP TELLS THE STORY
A Study in the Service of the Word

I grew up in Africa in a small village that was located in the middle of the forests of Zaire. The closest city was 150 miles away—and by American standards that city was no larger than a midwestern town.

My family lived isolated in that small forest compound, a place that had a name but was no more than an opening cut out of the dense forest. Obviously, it was not blessed with good communications—no bookstore or library, no radio or TV (I lived there before TV was invented), no phones, no telegraph—nothing. But I look back on those years with nostalgia. It was a wonderful place to grow up—primitive, close to nature, and part of a community.

African tribes are blessed with a good ancient form of communication—stories. I can still remember the Africans gathering around fires and telling the stories that communicated their sense of history and their values.

I can also remember that my dad came into my room every night (we lived in a mud home with a grass thatched roof like everybody else—except our home was square) to tell me a bedtime story—a story from the Bible. I loved those stories and would always beg, "Daddy, tell me another story." Everybody loves a good story. And what lies at the heart of Christian worship is a story.

THE NARRATIVE CHARACTER OF THE BIBLE

The African tribal story is not unlike the way the Bible was communicated and formed. The Near Eastern culture to which the story of God's saving work in history was entrusted was a storytelling community. The people of Israel told and retold the stories of God's working in their history. Those narratives were committed to writing and are in the Scripture for all to read and to tell.

Look at the entire Bible from the beginning to the end, and you will see that it is a story. We call it the story of redemption. It tells how we were created in God's image, how we fell away into sin, how God worked in history to restore our relationship to him. God worked through the patriarchs, through Israel, and through the prophets. Finally God came to us in the person of Jesus Christ who lived among us, was rejected and crucified for our sake, overcame the power of death by being resurrected from the dead, ascended into heaven, and will return again to restore the created order and make it new.

This story extends from Genesis to Revelation. And it is the story through which all the other stories of the Bible are to be understood.

Unfortunately, we often get lost in the particular stories of the Old Testament or the gospels. We want to know the moral of the story of Abraham or of Moses or of David or of the prodigal son. But, when we ask the "moral" question, we do a disservice to *the story*. The primary purpose of these stories is not to teach us morals or values (even though most do). Instead, they are all substories to the one great story, the story of God's redeeming love manifested ultimately in the incarnation, death, and resurrection of Jesus. They serve the larger story as part of the plot and action.

THE ENLIGHTENMENT

In the last three hundred years or so, the story base of the Scriptures and of worship, which retells the story, has been lost.

The Enlightenment, that period of time extending from 1600 to 1950, was a time of reason and proof. The "reign of reason," as some call it, turned the Bible into a series of propositions that were to be proven or debunked. The Scriptures were subjected to historical and scientific criticism. This approach to the Christian faith and to the Scriptures had a negative effect on worship. Let me explain.

In conservative circles, the Bible became a book to be proven. Conservative seminaries, using reason and science, sought to prove all the supernatural stories of the Bible with these tools. Consequently, they graduated students who walked into the pulpits of the world with the arguments for the faith—and turned worship into a time of teaching, persuasion, and proof of the validity of the Bible.

In more liberal circles the Bible became a book that had to be reinterpreted. It was argued that the supernatural stories could not possibly be true. Consequently, the liberals used the tools of reason and science to debunk the stories as myth. Nevertheless, they looked for a truth that stood behind the stories. Usually these were humanitarian truths or values by which people were to live their lives. Consequently, liberal preachers turned these biblical narratives into inspiring lessons for the growth and development of the human spirit.

In both cases—liberal and conservative—*the* story was lost.

Today, there is a return to the power of the story—to the message of redemption, salvation, and hope that is contained within *the* story and within all the stories of Scripture.

WORSHIP TELLS THE STORY

Worship, you might say, is the story in motion! The earliest description of Christian worship is found in Acts 2:42. In that passage we are told that the early Christians gathered around the "apostles' teaching."

This apostolic teaching has been identified in Christian scholarship as *kerygma* ("proclamation"). Scholarship has studied the kerygma, the proclamation of the early church in the sermons in the book of Acts, to determine its content. Primarily the content of the kerygma is The Story. Here are the elements of it:

- The time has been fulfilled.
- The Messiah has come.
- He was crucified, he was buried, and he rose from the dead.
- He has ascended into heaven, and he will return to earth to judge all evil.
- Repent, be baptized, and receive the Holy Spirit!
- The church is the new people of God.

Look closely at the heart of the early church proclamation. You can see at once that it is a story. But look again, and you can see how easily the story can become a matter of debate, an issue to be proved or disproved.

This story is the content of worship. In worship we recite the story, we proclaim the story, we sing the story, we feast to the story, and we are called to live out the story. The heart and substance of worship is *the* story.

THE SERVICE OF THE WORD

Take a moment to make a distinction in your mind between the acts of entrance and the service of the word.

The acts of entrance serve a different purpose. These acts bring you to the word and prepare you to hear the word. But the acts of worship in the service of the word are different. The service of the word recites and proclaims the story.

In the service of the word, we want to communicate the story of Scripture and tell the story of God's redeeming love in Jesus Christ. For this reason, the nature of the service of the word differs radically from the nature of the service of entrance. Here are the acts of the service of the word as they are ordered in the liturgical church:

+ Old Testament reading
+ Communal responsorial psalm
+ Epistle reading
+ Communal alleluia, canticle, hymn
+ Gospel reading
+ Sermon/Homily
+ Communal recitation of the creed
+ Prayers of the people
+ Passing of the peace

These acts of the service of the word can be shortened or adapted as the community wishes. But there are two things about this order that need to be preserved: (1) the emphasis on Scripture and (2) the participation of the congregation.

EMPHASIS ON SCRIPTURE

First, note how much Scripture is presented—an Old Testament lesson, a psalm, an epistle, and a gospel!

In most places of worship these Scriptures are read as printed in the text. But a new way to communicate the word has resulted from the communication revolution that has taken place recently.

We are all aware that we live in an audiovisual society. There is a great need in this day of television and visual communication to find new ways to communicate truth. Many churches are recognizing the need to communicate in ways that go beyond simply reading the Scripture. Here are some of the ways this is accomplished:

+ Storytelling the gospel
+ Dramatizing one of the texts
+ Creating a visual or visuals that enhance the text
+ Reading the Scripture with an accompanying pantomime or dance that expresses the story symbolically

PARTICIPATION OF THE CONGREGATION

Next, note the participation of the congregation in the responsorial psalm, the song between the epistle and the gospel, the saying of the creed, the prayers of the people, and the passing of the peace.

The people are *involved* in the action of the story as they *respond* to the story. The music of the responsorial psalm and the song between the epistle and the gospel are responses to the story. They need to be sung with enthusiasm and participation.

Some churches replace the creed with a "talk-back sermon." This kind of sermon is a brief response to the message. The people are simply asked to turn to one another and respond to what they have heard. What did it say to them? How did God speak to them or move them as they listened to the sermon?

Then the prayers of the people can be truly prayers "of the people." The prayer leader can bid the people to pray for the sick. The people can respond with the names of those in need. A similar approach to prayer can be taken regarding the needs of the church and of the world.

Finally, the passing of the peace brings the service of the word to an end and prepares the people to enter into the time of Communion, the giving of thanks for the death and resurrection of Jesus Christ. The peace is an expression of unity with the body of Christ. It says that we are reconciled with God and with each other. And it is done as people shake hands or embrace and say, "The peace of the Lord be with you."

CONCLUSION

In this session we have been examining the service of the word. What we encounter here in these acts of worship is the story of the Christian faith. The service of the word is the story of God's redeeming love expressed in recitation and proclamation. The cutting edge of worship renewal does not try to prove the story or debunk it or reinterpret it. Worship simply proclaims the story and brings the lives of people up into the story of redemption and hope.

STUDY GUIDE

Read Session 6, "Worship Tells the Story,"
before starting the study guide.

PART I: PERSONAL STUDY

Answer the following questions on your own.

1. *Life Connection*

♦ Can you remember a storyteller in your life? Try to recreate a situation in which you were told a good story. What was the story? What effect did it have in your life? Explain. _____

_____

_____

_____

_____

♦ The Scriptures tell a story—the story of how God rescues fallen creatures—and worship retells this story. Comment on your impression of *worship as story.* _____

_____

_____

_____

_____

_____

2. *Content Questions*

♦ Summarize in your own words the story of the Scriptures.

_____

_____

_____

_____

_____

◆ Explain why the stories of the Bible are not primarily moral stories, but stories that serve the overall redemptive story of the Bible. Give an example.

_____

_____

_____

_____

_____

◆ What did Enlightenment reason emphasize? How did this affect the story character of the Bible? _____

_____

_____

_____

_____

◆ How did the use of reason affect the conservative approach to the Bible and to worship? _____

_____

_____

_____

_____

◆ How did the use of reason affect the liberal approach to the Bible and to worship? _____

_____

_____

_____

_____

◆ Using your own words, write out the story line of the "apostles' teaching."

_____

_____

_____

_____

◆ What is the difference between the acts of entrance and the service of the word? _____

_____

_____

_____

_____

_____

_____

◆ In the column on the left side list the acts of worship found in the service of the word of a liturgical church. In the column on the right identify the "story element" that may be found in each of act.

Service of the word   Story element

_____   _____

_____   _____

_____   _____

_____   _____

_____   _____

_____   _____

_____   _____

_____   _____

◆ Read the story of the Emmaus road in Luke 24 and comment briefly how you would communicate this story, using the following forms of communication.

Storytelling _____

_____

Dramatizing the text _____

_____

Creating a visual to enhance the text_____

_____

Reading Scripture with an accompanying pantomime or dance _____

_____

- People need to respond to stories. In worship we respond to the story of Scripture in a number of ways. Comment on how each of the following may be seen as a response to the story of Scripture.

The responsorial psalm _____

A talk-back sermon _____

Prayers of the people _____

Passing of the peace_____

- In the space below suggest an order for the service of the word for your church. Write this order in the left column. In the right column suggest how you would communicate the story, for example, through drama, etc.

Service of the word   Way of communication

_____   _____

_____   _____

_____   _____

_____   _____

_____   _____

PART II: GROUP DISCUSSION

Write all of the group members' answers to the questions in each section on a chalkboard or flip chart.

1. *Life Connection*
- Begin by asking members of the group to share a story and the effect it had on their life.

2. *Thought Questions*
- Ask several members of the group to share their summary of the Scripture story.
- Explain why the stories of the Bible are not primarily moral stories.

- Define the Enlightenment and explain the impact it made in conservative and liberal circles.

- Have several members of the group present their summary of the story line of "apostles' teaching."

- Write the order of service from a traditional service of worship on the chalkboard or the flip chart and discuss it with the following questions.

- What are the acts of worship that express the story?

- What are the acts of worship that represent the response to the story?

- Do something creative with Luke 24. Divide the group into several smaller groups. Have one group present the text as a story; encourage another group to develop a drama; ask a third group to read a portion of the passage with an accompanying pantomime or dance.

- Take some time to discuss the communications revolution—the shift from a text-oriented society to an audiovisual society. How has this revolution impacted on the communication of God's word in worship?

WORSHIP CELEBRATES THE FEAST

A Study in the Lord's Supper

I think all of us have vivid memories from our childhood. Because I grew up in Africa, my memories are quite distinct and reflect geographical areas, cultures, and customs that are very different from my American heritage.

I can still remember the African feasts, for example. Even though the village that my parents served as missionaries was a poor place where people eked a living out of the land and the forest, people knew how to feast. The exquisite food, the brightly colored clothing, the dancing, and the singing made the African feast a special occasion that I remember vividly.

Feasting also lies at the heart of Christian worship. Let's go back and look at the origin of feasting in the early church.

THE NEW TESTAMENT FEAST

We have already seen the earliest description of Christian worship in Acts 2:42–47. The two central foci of Christian worship are stated in verse 42—the apostolic teaching and the breaking of bread. In this session I want to address the breaking of the bread, a festal occasion for the early Christians. In order to do so I must tell you two stories—the first about the Jewish Shabbat and the second about the postresurrection appearance of Jesus. These two stories will give us insight into the experience of the early Christians at the table of the Lord—what we call in our various traditions the breaking of the bread, the Lord's Supper, the Communion, the Eucharist.

First the Shabbat story. The story I am going to tell you is a modern story, but it gives you insight into a Jewish practice that goes back to the time of Jesus—a practice that was in the experience and the memory of the early Christians who came to receive the bread and wine at the breaking of the bread.

SHABBAT AND THE EARLY CHRISTIAN EXPERIENCE
AT THE TABLE OF THE LORD

A number of years ago I became friends with Rabbi Yechiel Eckstein through the Chicago area evangelical and Jewish dialogue. Yechiel, who is the president of the Holy Land Fellowship and author of the highly acclaimed book *What Every Christian Should Know about Jews and Judaism,* invited my colleague Morris Inch, myself, and our wives to celebrate Shabbat with them.

Yechiel gave us directions to his home, but he said, "If you get lost don't call, because we don't answer our phone after sunset on Friday. We rest, we really rest."

When we arrived at the door, Yechiel's lovely wife, Bonnie, enthusiastically greeted us all with an embrace and made us feel at home immediately. As we were taking off our coats, she pointed to a number of candles burning at a side table. "Four of those candles represent our family," she said, "and each of the other four is lighted in honor of your presence." I felt welcome!

After a brief time of friendly conversation, we were invited to sit down at the table. Yechiel sat at one end, Bonnie at the other, the two couples on either side, and the children on both sides of their mother. As I pulled my chair in behind me, I wondered what kind of prayer would precede our feast.

"This is a very special meal," Yechiel said, "not only because you are here, but because this meal represents the beginning of our Jewish Shabbat. It's a day of rest, a time to remember our Creator and Redeemer, a time to be with the family, a time to establish and deepen our relationships. Some of our table prayers will be said in Hebrew. Just relax and enter the spirit of our thanksgiving."

As Yechiel began praising God in Hebrew for bringing forth food from the earth, he took a small loaf of freshly baked bread, broke it, and passed it around the table, bidding us to eat as a sign of our thanks to God. Again, pouring wine into a cup, he lifted it, repeating a Jewish prayer of thanks for the fruit of the vine and, passing it around the table, bade us drink as a sign of our thanks to God. After another prayer our meal began.

As we were eating the delicious food that had been prepared before sundown and kept warm in the oven (no cooking is allowed after sundown), we engaged in a conversation that was more than talk. It was communication—about our lives, our families, our values, our dreams.

After dessert, Yechiel said, "In our tradition we conclude the Shabbat meal with more table prayers and psalms. All of this will be done in Hebrew, so simply join in the spirit of what we do." We all bowed our heads. A softly sung litany was begun as Yechiel and Bonnie took turns singing prayers and psalms. Although I could not understand the language, the sense of awe and reverence before the Lord came over me and raised my spirits to the praise of God. After the prayers ended, Yechiel looked at Bonnie and in English spoke of his love for her and of his good fortune in having her as his wife. Then, calling his children to his side, he placed his hands on their heads and, blessing them, sent them happily off to play.

During the meal, on the way home, and for weeks afterward, I reflected on that event. What we were involved in was more than a meal, it was a ritual—a religious ritual—that had *power* to unite a family, recall history, create reverential awe, shape values, and provide a focal point to which memory for both parents and children will return again and again.

Through this experience I was reminded once again that the richness of the Jewish tradition is the heritage of the Christian family. But for many of us this heritage has been lost or has fallen into the background. Let me explain.

I do not mean to suggest that most Christian homes don't have prayer at meals or prayers for children at bedtime or even regular family prayer. What I mean to say is that most of us do not have table prayers that sanctify time or set apart special occasions and turn them into spiritual festivals that communicate the sense of lifting the event into the very presence of God.

The meal prayers at Rabbi Eckstein's entered us into Sabbath rest. This was no ordinary evening; it was an extraordinary event that turned a meal into a religious experience.

We have to ask ourselves, What is significant about this experience? Yechiel gave me a clue that evening when he said to me, "You know, Bob, we Jews love the Sabbath. It is a time for rest, and a time to spend renewing our relationship to God, to family, and to friends."

Eating together establishes, maintains, repairs, and always transforms relationships. In the early church the new Christian from a Jewish background took the expectation of relationship to the breaking of the bread.

But the next question—and the one that leads us into the next story—is, Relationship with whom?

THE EMMAUS ROAD EXPERIENCE

The best way to answer this question is to reread the story of Cleopas and his wife (his companion is not named, but it is reasonable to assume it was his wife) on the road to Emmaus, recorded in Luke 24:13–32.

Space does not permit a full retelling of the story, so stop reading this lesson and take a few moments to read the Scripture text. Then reflect on these key points:

- Cleopas and his wife feel fully dislocated because of losing their friend, companion, and Messiah to a cruel death on the cross.
- On Sunday after the crucifixion they are walking home, fully discouraged and attempting to interpret the events of the weekend, when a stranger appears and walks with them.
- First, the stranger interprets the Old Testament to them in a new way, and their hearts burn with a new fire.
- Next, the stranger comes into their home to eat with them. At the table he takes the bread, breaks it, and gives them some. Then they see who it is—it is the *resurrected* Jesus! All of a sudden, life becomes new, and they are relocated in God!
- Full of faith, they run back to Jerusalem to tell the disciples.

Note the words Luke uses to capture their communication: "Then the two told what had happened on the way, and how Jesus was recognized by them when he broke the bread" (v. 35).

How do these two stories relate to feast in the experience of the early church?

FEAST IN THE EARLY CHURCH

These two stories give us enormous insight into the worship of the early church. Scholars of worship have shown that the breaking of the bread was an agape ("love") feast. Our stories essentially tell us that the early Christians came to this agape feast with *an expectation of relationship with the resurrected Jesus who was present at the feast.*

The breaking of the bread was not a dour, sober experience of the death of Jesus, but a wonderful celebration and feast of the resurrection!

You may be saying, "Okay, I agree with you. Worship at the table of the Lord should be more joyful—but how do you do it? How do I as a worship leader break with the passive and sober approach to the table?"

A SUGGESTED APPROACH

Let me make four suggestions.

First, improve the prayer of thanksgiving over the bread and wine. Every worship leader says some kind of prayer over the bread and wine, usually a prayer thanking

God for the death of God's Son and for the salvation that comes from the broken body and shed blood. The content of this prayer can be expanded and enhanced by following an order of the prayer of thanksgiving that was used in the ancient church and is still used in many churches today. This ancient order derives from the Jewish *Berakah* ("blessing") prayers that included a prayer of praise, a prayer of commemoration, and a prayer of petition. When you stand before the people and pray a prayer of thanksgiving over the bread and wine, simply follow the ancient tradition.

- Praise God for the work of the Son and express the desire to join with the angels, the archangels, the cherubim, and the seraphim who stand around the throne of God singing, "Holy, Holy, Holy." (The congregation may join in singing one of the many versions of this song.)
- Give thanks for God's mighty deeds of salvation by briefly reciting the history of God's acts of salvation expressed throughout the Old Testament and in the death and resurrection of Jesus. Conclude this prayer with the words of Jesus in Matthew 26:26–28, the breaking of the bread, and the pouring or lifting of the cup.
- Ask God to bless the congregation with the fullness of the Holy Spirit and the confirmation of faith. These words may be followed by the invitation to receive the bread and wine.

Second, invite the people to come forward to receive the bread and wine. Worship renewal emphasizes participation and involvement. By asking the people to stand, walk down the aisle, and receive the bread and then the wine, you are inviting them to say yes again to the death and resurrection.

Third, while the people are coming to receive the bread and wine, sing! Singing breaks through the passive character of the Lord's table as it is observed in many churches. It allows the whole community of faith to express the mystery of faith and the joy of Christ's saving and healing presence at the table. Sing three kinds of songs—songs of the death of the Lord, songs of his resurrection, and finally songs of his exaltation. This progression of songs orders the experience of the worshiping church past the death (where too many churches remain) into the joy of the resurrection and exaltation.

Finally, provide a time of ministry with the anointing of oil and the laying on of hands for healing and empowerment. This act of ministry extends the meaning of the death and resurrection—God's acts of salvation and healing—and allows the congregation to experience the power of Christ's death and resurrection.

In conclusion, let me say once again that our worship needs to strive toward biblical fullness, and this means more frequent celebration of the table. But what worship renewal is experiencing is not the old funeral approach to the table, but a powerful, joyful experience of the resurrected Christ who is present at bread and wine to touch, to heal, and to make whole. This is celebration worship.

CONCLUSION

We have seen that worship at the table needs renewal in most of our traditions. In particular we need to consider more frequent celebration of the table and imbuing our worship at the table of the Lord with the spirit of celebration!

STUDY GUIDE

Read Session 7, "Worship Celebrates the Feast,"
before starting the study guide.

PART I: PERSONAL STUDY

Answer the following questions on your own.

1. *Life Connection*
  - Describe one of the most significant feasts of your life. _____
  _____
  _____
  _____
  _____
  _____
  _____
  _____
  _____

  - How did this feast make an impact on your life? _____
  _____
  _____
  _____
  _____
  _____
  _____

2. *Content Questions*
  - What is so important about the Jewish Shabbat feast? _____
  _____
  _____
  _____
  _____
  _____
  _____

◆ Give an example from your own life that illustrates the truth of this statement: Eating together establishes, maintains, repairs, and transforms relationships. _____

_____

_____

_____

_____

◆ Read Luke 24. Explain the role that eating played in establishing the relationship of Cleopas and his wife with Jesus. _____

_____

_____

_____

_____

◆ Explain the agape feast in the early church. _____

_____

_____

_____

_____

◆ Explain this statement: The early Christians came to the agape feast with an expectation of relationship with the risen Christ._____

_____

_____

_____

_____

◆ Describe the mood of the agape feast: _____

_____

_____

_____

_____

◆ Explain the three parts of the prayer of thanksgiving over bread and wine used in the ancient church.

a. _____

_____

b. _____

_____

c. _____

_____

◆ What is the value of people coming forward to receive the bread and wine? _____

_____

_____

_____

_____

◆ What kinds of songs should be sung during Communion?

_____

_____

_____

_____

◆ What kind of ministry may be provided during the Communion time?

_____

_____

_____

_____

3. *Application*

◆ Which of the following characterize the Communion service in your church?

❏ A prayer of thanksgiving is said over the bread and wine.

❏ We sing during the reception of bread and wine.

❏ During the reception of bread and wine people are anointed with oil for healing in mind, body, and spirit.

❏ Communion is a time of great joy.

◆ Describe the Communion service in your church, using your own words.

_____

_____

_____

_____

◆ If you were to make a change in the celebration of Communion in your church, what would it be? _____

_____

_____

_____

_____

◆ Write a prayer of thanksgiving for Communion that follows the ancient pattern of praise, commemoration, and petition.

_____

_____

_____

_____

_____

◆ Write a suggested order of worship for Communion in your church.

_____

_____

_____

_____

_____

PART II: GROUP DISCUSSION

Write all of the group members' answers to the questions in each section on a chalkboard or flip chart.

1. *Life Connection*

◆ Begin by asking several members of the group to tell about the most significant feast in their lives. Probe how this feast may have influenced their lives.

2. *Thought Questions*

♦ Ask if any members of the group have ever eaten in a Jewish home, particularly on the Friday night Shabbat. Have them describe their experience.

♦ Ask if someone can provide an example from personal experience that verifies that "eating establishes, maintains, repairs, and transforms relationships."

♦ How is the above statement reflected in the story of Cleopas and his companion (wife)?

♦ How many different Christian denominations or traditions have people in this group experienced? Describe Communion in these traditions.

♦ Ask, "Has anyone here experienced a Christian agape feast? How would you compare the early Christian agape feast to a church potluck?"

3. *Application*

♦ How would you characterize the Communion service in this church? Sober? Celebratory? Central to worship? Joyful? Meaningful? Boring? Dead?

♦ Ask several people to share the Communion prayer they wrote.

♦ Ask several people to share the order of Communion they have prepared.

♦ What kind of changes would you like to see in the Communion practice of this church?

WORSHIP SENDS THE PEOPLE FORTH

A Study in the Acts of Dismissal

 In Session 3 I told how Andrew Greeley once described Christian worship during a radio interview: "We gather the people, tell the story, break bread, and go home."

This simple but direct answer summarizes what we have been discussing in the last several sessions—the fourfold pattern of coming before the Lord. Now we will examine the last of the four actions.

Going home—or better put, going forth—is no simple action. It's not like, "Worship is ended, go home!" or, "Worship is over, let's get on with our lives." It's much more than that.

THE MEANING OF GOING FORTH

Paul captures the real meaning of being sent forth when he writes to the Roman Christians, "Therefore, I urge you, brothers, in view of God's mercy, to offer your bodies as living sacrifices, holy and pleasing to God—this is your spiritual act of worship" (Rom 12:1). Paul is saying that worship is a way of life. Rather than ending at the door of the church, worship continues into every aspect of our lives—our homes, our work, our recreation.

In the Episcopal *Book of Common Prayer*, the service ends with the minister saying, "Go forth into the world to love and serve the Lord," to which the people enthusiastically respond, "Thanks be to God." The Catholic *Constitution on the Sacred Liturgy* poignantly says, "the liturgy is the summit toward which the activity of the Church is directed; it is also the fount from which all her power flows" (1.10). These two documents capture the Pauline concept that worship extends to all of life and to all that we do. For this reason, we need to think clearly about what we do when we send the people forth.

What Does the Dismissal Do?

If we want the dismissal in worship to mean more to the worshiper, we need to begin by asking the simple question, What does the dismissal do?

Primarily, the dismissal is a blessing.

The word *blessing* has many uses. In worship, we actually bless God when we offer praise and worship. To bless God means that we pronounce or confer upon God the wonder and might of God's own name. In the ancient St. John Chrysostom liturgy (AD 380), the opening sentences of the Eucharistic liturgy include these words of blessing, "It is fitting and right to sing to you, to bless you, to praise you, to give thanks to you, to worship you in every place of your dominion. For you are God beyond description, beyond understanding, invisible, incomprehensible, always existing, always the same; you and your only-begotten Son and your Holy Spirit." When we worship God for who God is, it blesses and pleases God.

When we bless God through our praise and worship, however, we do not confer anything on God. Rather, we bless God by offering what is pleasing to God—acknowledgment and service.

On the other hand, when God blesses us, he confers on us a power to fulfill our calling in righteousness and our holiness in Jesus Christ. God's blessing on us is a gift—an undeserved, unmerited divine favor.

The origin of the dismissal blessing lies in the Old Testament, in what is often called the "Aaronic blessing":

> The LORD said to Moses, "Tell Aaron and his sons, 'This is how you are to bless the Israelites. Say to them: "The LORD bless you and keep you; the LORD make his face shine upon you and be gracious to you; the LORD turn his face toward you and give you peace." ' So they will put my name on the Israelites, and I will bless them" (Num 6:22–27).

The key to this and all blessings is found in the beginning of the last phrase: "So they will put *my name* on the Israelites" [author's emphasis]. In a blessing, God confers his own name on us, and *that's how we are to live our lives.* I wonder how our lives would change if, in every detail of our daily life, we consciously recognized that we have the name of God upon us.

Suggestions for Dismissal

The ordinary rites of dismissal include three acts:

* the benediction (God's blessing)

- a dismissal hymn (a hymn or gospel song that sends the people forth with a mission)
- words of dismissal, such as:

Minister: "Go forth into the world to love and serve the Lord."
People: "Thanks be to God."

A recent, and I think healthy, trend in dismissal blessings is to tie the words of the dismissal into concrete examples in the lives of the people. The best way to do this is to think of the people you actually know in the congregation and use their work and lives as an example. More than likely, a number of people have similar work or household responsibilities. Here, for example, is a specific adaptation of the Aaronic blessing:

The Lord bless you and keep you: May relationships at home and at the office be healed and strengthened.

The Lord make his face to shine upon you, and be gracious to you: May God give you good health, vigor, and stamina in all you do.

The Lord lift his countenance upon you, and give you peace: May you rest well, be encouraged in your work, and be at peace with your neighbor.

In the name of the Father, the Son, and the Holy Spirit.

CONCLUSION

This session has considered the significance of the dismissal. As you continue to think about, pray about, and experiment with the dismissal, may God bless you, your planning, and your dismissing. And may the people go forth with the sense that God's name is upon them and upon all they do.

STUDY GUIDE

*Read Session 8, "Worship Sends the People Forth to Serve,"
before starting the study guide.*

PART I: PERSONAL STUDY

Answer the following questions on your own.

1. *Life Connection*

♦ Take some time to think about the idea of "going forth." What important meeting have you attended lately (other than a worship service) where you were challenged to do something important? Describe that occasion and how it felt to go forth with a mission in your mind and heart.

_____

_____

_____

_____

_____

♦ Describe a worship service or a religious gathering where you experienced a challenge to go forth. How did you feel about what you were sent forth to do or to be? _____

_____

_____

_____

_____

_____

2. *Thought Questions*

♦ Read Romans 12:1. Use your own words to describe how this text relates to the idea of "going forth." _____

_____

_____

_____

_____

• These words are found in the *Book of Common Prayer:* "Go forth into the world to love and serve the Lord." The following questions ask you to list the many ways you can serve the Lord in various areas of your life.

How I can serve the Lord in my personal, private life _____

_____

_____

_____

How I can serve the Lord in my family life_____

_____

_____

_____

How I can serve the Lord in my work _____

_____

_____

_____

• These words are found in the *Constitution on the Sacred Liturgy:* "The liturgy is the summit toward which the activity of the church is directed; it is also the fount from which all her power flows." In the space below draw an hourglass on its side. Write the word "worship" at the neck of the hourglass. In the space on the left write down all the activities of the church that are directed toward worship. On the right side write down all the ministries of the church that are empowered by worship.

◆ What does the dismissal do? _____

_____

_____

◆ What does it mean to bless God? _____

_____

_____

_____

_____

◆ The opening sentences of the Eucharistic portion of the St. John Chrysostom liturgy include words of blessing, which are listed below. Indicate
how you fulfill the spiritual meaning of these words in the way you worship God in your life.

To sing to you _____

_____

To bless you _____

_____

To praise you _____

_____

To give thanks to you _____

_____

To worship you _____

_____

in every place of your dominion _____

_____

◆ What does God confer on us through the blessing, or the benediction?

_____

_____

_____

_____

_____

_____

_____

3. *Application*

♦ Below are the words of the "Aaronic blessing" (Num 6:22–27). How would you apply these blessings to specifics in your life? Name specific situations and desires. Make it your personal blessing prayer.

The Lord bless you and keep you _____

_____

The Lord make his face shine upon you _____

_____

And be gracious to you _____

_____

The Lord turn his face toward you _____

_____

And give you peace _____

_____

[The Lord] put [his] name on you _____

_____

And bless you _____

_____

♦ Having learned about the structure and importance of the dismissal, write a dismissal that you would like to be used in the worship of your church.

_____

_____

_____

_____

PART II: GROUP DISCUSSION

Write all of the group members' answers to the questions in each section on the chalkboard or flip chart.

1. *Life Connection*

♦ Begin the group study by asking several members of the group to share an important meeting in which they felt challenged and empowered to "go forth" and accomplish something.

2. *Content Questions*

- Read Romans 12:1 and ask for the various interpretations of this passage that were developed by the group.

- Ask several members of the group to share their application of the words "go forth into the world to love and serve the Lord" in their (1) personal life, (2) family life, and (3) work.

- Draw an hourglass on the chalkboard or flip chart and discuss the ways in which the church can better understand the implications of the statement from the *Constitution on the Liturgy*: "The liturgy is the summit toward which the activity of the Church is directed; it is also the fount from which all her power flows." What are the activities of the church that flow into worship? What are the activities of the church that worship empowers?

- Ask members of the group to share the way in which they desire to fulfill the spiritual meaning of the words of the St. John Chrysostom liturgy in the way in which they live in the world: "To sing to you, to bless you, to praise you, to give thanks to you, to worship you in every place of your dominion."

3. *Application*

- Read the Aaronic blessing (Num 6:22–27) and ask group members to respond by stating how they desire God to apply these blessings to specifics in their lives.

- Ask members of the group to present the specific prayers of benediction they wrote for worship.

- Discuss how the benediction in the worship of your church may be improved.

PART III

BREAKING THROUGH THE BARRIERS OF PASSIVE WORSHIP

WOUNDS THAT HINDER WORSHIP

A Study in the Psychology of Worship

 I work with local congregations in the field of worship, and people ask me many questions. One that comes up from time to time is, I just can't seem to worship. Is something wrong with me?

This is a difficult question to answer. Someone may not feel free to worship because the pastor or worship leader has a wooden, rote, or controlling manner that does not give permission to worship. Another person may not feel free to worship because of emotional wounds that are damaging to freedom of expression. These persons may worship with the intellect, but their capacity for affective worship is impaired. They want to feel what they understand. But they can't. This session explores the problem of wounds that hinder a full and free participation in worship.

ORIGINS OF WOUNDEDNESS

Usually the wounds that hinder worship are traceable to childhood experiences. These negative experiences, which derive from unhealthy relationships or traumatic events, form patterns of behavior that hinder the flow and expression of normal emotional behavior. Such experiences include

- the divorce of parents
- physical or sexual abuse
- an alcoholic parent
- abandonment and neglect
- conditional love based on performance
- a home filled with strife and disunity
- emotional abuse
- harsh and inconsistent discipline

Children who are raised in situations like those described above often have two minds: the adult conceptual or rational mind and the childlike emotional or experiential mind. For example, the adult conceptual mind may understand the joy of standing in the presence of God and offering worship to God. But because the child within the adult has never experienced the joy of relationship with the parent (having experienced mostly judgment and rejection), the child within is not able to experience the joy and thanksgiving of worship. Consequently, in worship there is a divorce between an intellectual understanding of praise and the actual experience of praise. A healthy psyche can experience both, but a wounded psyche may only understand with the intellect and not be able to experience with the emotions.

HOW WOUNDEDNESS IS EXPRESSED

Psychologists speak of personality in terms of mind, will, and emotion. Personal woundedness in any of these three areas can hinder our ability to enter fully into the experience of worship.

The wounding of the mind is usually expressed in negative thoughts and attitudes. The wounded person lives with the uneasy feeling that something is wrong. They tend to blame themselves or someone else. In worship this wounded-ness shows up in a habitual attitude of criticism; in frustration with those in authority; in dissatisfaction with the way things are done; and in a sense of guilt and unworthiness and a belief that others are critical and disproving.

When woundedness affects the will, it usually shows up in a constant struggle with discipline. This worshiper frequently resolves to be in worship on a regular basis, but fails to keep those resolutions. In addition, there is an attention deficit in worship itself. The desire may be there to listen, to respond, to be involved. But in fact, the desire is expressed in a half-hearted approach to and experience of worship.

Persons who are damaged in their emotions are usually unable to achieve intimacy with God in worship. For them, a relationship with God is primarily intellectual. They have a conceptual knowledge of the fruits of a good relation-ship—love, joy, peace—but their experience of worship is dry and empty. They look on those who speak of the refreshment and power of the worship experience with a sense of amazement and frustration. They want intimacy but can't experience it, no matter how hard they try. Consequently, worship often results in a sense of sadness or even anger.

REACTIONS TO WOUNDEDNESS

Wounded people who come to worship and attempt to experience God in worship may respond to their inability to worship and experience intimacy with God in a number of ways.

A person may completely give up and drop away from the church and from faith in God all together. After months, perhaps years of attempting to have a personal relationship with God, he or she may conclude that God does not exist or that God has rejected him or her.

Others may stay faithful in attendance, but keep themselves safe from intimacy by remaining uninvolved. Because they do not want to risk rejection, they remain on the edge of the community. They may attend worship on a regular basis, but they don't get involved. It is enough for them to show up at worship and then go home.

Some deal with their woundedness by church-hopping. When the challenge of a relationship becomes intense, these people may simply withdraw and go to another church where they feel safe again.

Others treat their woundedness by retreating behind a convenient mask. They wear a facade of joy, love, and relationship and in this way hide their woundedness to others and sometimes even to themselves. They may burn out and drop away from church or fall into sin that reveals their wounds. Sometimes they maintain the appearance of an outwardly strong spiritual life, but their inner spiritual self is empty and shallow.

Some respond to their woundedness by going on the attack. For them, nothing is done right and there is always someone to blame. Still others attempt to control. Because their own inner life is out of control, they attempt to get a handle on things by seeking to control others.

HOW TO CHANGE

Those who have been wounded will never be able to experience the fullness of worship until they have dealt with their woundedness. Dealing with woundedness is no easy journey, but it is one that can be taken by following several careful but often painful steps.

The first step is self-discovery. The wounded person needs to go back to childhood and discover those wounds that hinder the full experience of personality in worship, as well as in other areas of life. He or she needs to rediscover and to confront childhood decisions that remain hidden from the adult mind. For example, the child may have said, I will never get close enough for someone to hurt me like that again, or, People will always leave me, so it won't hurt as much if I leave them first, or, No one will ever love me, or, You can't trust anyone. All these beliefs must be replaced in order for the wounds to heal. In the process of dealing with these hurts, the feelings of the child will surface. While the experience of these feelings will not bring healing, healing cannot occur until the feelings have been dealt with.

The next step is to form safe relationships in which childhood feelings can be shared. This can happen with a counselor, a trusted friend, or a small group of caring people. Many churches have small groups that can function as a caring, listening community.

Next, the wounded person needs to move toward forgiveness and restoration. In order to accomplish this step, the wounded person needs to sort out the source of woundedness to know who was responsible for what. Blame is often placed upon others, but sometimes some of the blame must be laid at the feet of the wounded. Consequently, it is a complicated matter to sort out who must be forgiven and what the wounded person needs to forgive in himself or herself. Once this matter has been taken care of as much as possible, the wounded person must move to establish restoration with those involved. Often the church is able to help in the process of reconciliation through a formal or informal process that may involve the pastor or mediator in a counseling setting or in a ritual of reconciliation.

The final step that the wounded person must take is changing his or her behavior. The goal is to replace old patterns of behavior with new patterns. This involves *understanding* the old patterns and *establishing* new patterns through the long process of trial and error. A considerable amount of time and compassionate support by others is needed to make lasting changes that result in healing.

CONCLUSION

As healing begins to occur, the experience of worship begins to change. A new sense of trust in God will grow, as well as a feeling of belonging to the worshiping community. Words and actions of worship that are already familiar will begin to take on new meaning, and an overwhelming experience of gratitude toward God will occur. As the emotional, affective side of the person comes alive, intimacy with God and others develops. (This chapter is based on Margaret Webb, "Wounds That Hinder Worship," in *The Complete Library of Christian Worship*, vol. 3, *The Renewal of Sunday Worship*, pp. 381–86.)

STUDY GUIDE

Read Sessiom 9, "Wounds That Hinder Worship,"
before starting the study guide.

PART I: PERSONAL STUDY

Answer the following questions on your own. (These questions may be very personal. Skip any that make you feel uncomfortable.)

1. *Life Connection*

◆ Did you see something about yourself in this study of woundedness? Have you been wounded in any way that may affect your experience of worship? If so, express your self-understanding in the space below.

_____

_____

_____

_____

◆ Did this session help you understand the behavior of someone else (preferably not in the same church)? Summarize the behavior of that person that may indicate woundedness. _____

_____

_____

_____

_____

2. *Thought Questions*

◆ Have you experienced any wounds in life that may inhibit your ability to achieve intimacy with God and your fellow worshiper? ❑ Yes ❑ No

◆ Which of the following wounds have you experienced, either in childhood or in your adult years?
   ❑ Parents' divorce
   ❑ Physical or sexual abuse
   ❑ Alcoholic parent(s)

❑ Abandonment or neglect
❑ Conditional love based on performance
❑ A home filled with strife and disunity
❑ Emotional abuse
❑ Harsh and inconsistent discipline

♦ Do you fit the profile of the person with an adult conceptual mind and a childlike emotional makeup? That is, do you *understand* worship better than you *experience* worship? ❑ Yes ❑ No
Comment: _____

_____

_____

_____

_____

♦ Do you experience any of the characteristics of a wounded mind? Check the ones that you experience.
❑ A habitual attitude of criticism
❑ Frustration with authority
❑ Dissatisfaction with the way things are done
❑ A sense of guilt and unworthiness
❑ A feeling that others disapprove of you

♦ Woundedness of the will usually shows up in a constant struggle with discipline. Do you experience this battle? ❑ Yes ❑ No

♦ Do you experience any of the characteristics of damaged emotions? Check the ones you experience.
❑ A relationship with God that is primarily intellectual
❑ A conceptual knowledge of love, joy, and peace, but no experience of those feelings
❑ Envy toward those who speak of the refreshment and power of worship
❑ A failure to achieve intimacy

♦ Do you experience any of these reactions to woundedness?
❑ Church and worship dropout
❑ An uninvolved relationship with the church and worship
❑ Church hopping
❑ Retreating behind a mask

❑ Attacking others for not doing things right
❑ Attempting to control others

• On the basis of the questions above, how would you describe yourself?
  ❑ Wounded
  ❑ Healthy
  ❑ Somewhere in between

3. *Application*

• Take some time to think through your childhood. Are you able to get in contact with any negative experiences that may have wounded you? If so, take some time to write a self-discovery. _____

_____

_____

_____

_____

_____

• The next step in healing is to establish safe relationships. Comment on the safe relationship you have or will make._____

_____

_____

_____

_____

_____

• The next step is forgiveness and restoration. Give an example of how both forgiveness and restoration have taken place in your life. If the process of forgiveness and restoration is now occurring, comment on that process. _____

_____

_____

_____

_____

_____

♦ If you have completed the process of restoration, explain how this achievement has affected your experience of worship. _____

_____

_____

_____

_____

PART II: GROUP DISCUSSION

Write all of the group members' answers to the questions in each section on a chalkboard or flip chart. Because the content of the questions is so personal, be especially sensitive to each student's experience.

1. *Life Connection*

♦ Begin the group discussion by asking several members of the group to share an experience that resulted in wounds listed under the thought questions of the individual study. *Do not push any of the students to talk about an experience that resulted in woundedness from one of these specific situations.* If a person *wants* to talk, listen with compassion.

♦ Ask for examples from those who feel they have the characteristics of a wounded mind.

♦ Ask for examples from those who feel they have the characteristics of a wounded will.

♦ Ask for examples of those who have the characteristics of damaged emotions.

♦ Walk through the examples of reactions to woundedness. Has anyone experienced one or more of these reactions?

2. *Application*

♦ Ask for examples of those who experienced *self-discovery* through woundedness. How did they discover their woundedness? How would they help another discover woundedness?

♦ Ask those who are in safe relationships to describe their experience. Does this church provide safe small groups where people can establish new relationships that can bring healing to woundedness?

- Ask those who have experienced forgiveness and restoration to speak of their experience. Does this church provide a setting or ritual for restoration? How does it work?
- Ask those who have completed an experience of restoration to comment on how it has changed or influenced their experience of worship.

PRAYER THAT INVOLVES THE CONGREGATION

A Study in the Prayers of Worship

Many years ago, when I was in the third grade, my father was the pastor of two small churches in the Pocono area of Pennsylvania. I have many memories of my year in that place—some from the surrounding area, some from the home in which we lived, some from school, and some from the churches.

My most distinct memory from the churches is the time we spent together in prayer. The tradition of one of the churches was to pray in unison. When the time came for the prayers of the people, my dad would announce some prayer requests and then say, "Let us go to prayer." These words were a signal for all the people to go to their knees, their bodies turned so they were facing the back of their own pew. And then, without further announcement, all the people would pray at once and out loud. A chorus of voices filled that room with their requests. When the prayers slowed down, my dad would pray a prayer that brought the prayer time to a close.

I don't think I have experienced the unison approach to prayer in any other church, but one of my students recently visited a church that uses this approach, so the tradition survives.

In this session we will look at prayer in worship and ask how we can get the congregation involved.

PRAYER IN WORSHIP

Worship includes prayers that are not said by the congregation. However, each person should pray along with the spoken prayer, using the ear and the heart. By listening with intention, each person participates in the prayer generally led by the pastor or worship leader. I want to mention these prayers and then go on to concentrate on the prayers of the people.

The prayers of gathering are generally prayed by the leader of worship. The first of these prayers is called an invocation. This prayer invokes the worship of the people. The best known prayer of invocation, which is prayed with some variation in many churches around the world, is as follows:

Almighty God, to you all hearts are open, all desires known, and from you no secrets are hid: Cleanse the thoughts of our hearts by the inspiration of your Holy Spirit, that we may perfectly love you, and worthily magnify your holy Name; through Christ our Lord. Amen.

THE COLLECT

In liturgical churches the acts of entrance conclude with a "collect" (which means to collect the prayers of the people) that serves as a transition to the service of the word. The words of the collect always center on the particular day of the Christian year and the theme or the texts of the service. Here, for example, is a collect for the first Sunday after Christmas:

Almighty God, you have poured upon us the new light of your incarnate Word: Grant that this light, enkindled in our hearts, may shine forth in our lives; through Jesus Christ our Lord, who lives and reigns with you, in the unity of the Holy Spirit, one God, now and forever. Amen.

The sentiment of this prayer is echoed in free church and contemporary worship as well. The worship leader who is mindful of the theme of the day will pray similar thoughts, but in an extemporaneous manner.

THE PRAYER OF CONFESSION

A third kind of prayer that is sometimes in the acts of entrance, but more usually in the service of the word (after the prayers of the people), is the prayer of confession. This prayer is prayed by all the people in unison. It concludes the prayers of the people and prepares the people to receive the Eucharist. Here is that prayer from the liturgical tradition:

Most merciful God,
we confess that we have sinned against you
in thought, word, and deed,
by what we have done,
and by what we have left undone.
We have not loved you with our whole heart;

we have not loved our neighbors as ourselves.
We are truly sorry and we humbly repent.
For the sake of your Son Jesus Christ,
have mercy on us and forgive us;
that we may delight in your will,
and walk in your ways,
to the glory of your Name. Amen.

While churches of the free tradition do not pray the specific words of this prayer, they do pray the sentiment. Many free churches do not have prayers of confession every Sunday, but they normally have them on those days when the Lord's Supper is celebrated. Often the prayer of confession is done in a time of silence and personal meditation.

THE EUCHARISTIC PRAYER

Then there is the Eucharistic prayer. In liturgical churches, the prayers said at the table of the Lord combine a prayer of adoration (the Father), a prayer of thanksgiving (for the work of the Son), and a prayer of invocation, or "epiclesis" (a petition to the Holy Spirit to be present to the people). The Eucharistic prayer may also contain a prayer of remembrance and offering, depending on the tradition.

In liturgical churches a written text is followed for these prayers. In the free church tradition similar prayers may be offered at the table of the Lord, but they are done in an extemporaneous manner.

These approaches to prayer in worship have been established through history and reach all the way back to the early church. All of these prayers, with the exception of the prayer of confession, are spoken by the leadership.

We turn now to the "prayers of the people"—prayers that are said by the people in worship.

THE PRAYERS OF THE PEOPLE

The "prayers of the people" represents a style of congregational prayer that originated in the early church. In many churches these prayers have been supplanted by the pastoral prayer. Unfortunately, the pastoral prayer, prayed by the pastor on behalf of the people, takes the action of prayer away from the people. In contemporary renewal worship the prayers of the people are being restored.

Petition is not the exclusive work of the pastor. It is the work of the entire body of Christ and is best performed by the whole church.

In the early church, the prayers of the people were conducted in a certain way. The deacon announced a matter of prayer, and then the people prayed for this matter out loud and in unison. Then another matter of prayer was announced, and so on.

Eventually a formal plan for this prayer was set forth in the liturgies of the early church. Gregory Dix, in his work *The Shape of the Liturgy* (London: Dacre, 1975), provides us with this description of the people's prayer from the early church:

> First, a subject was announced, either by the officiant (in the West) or the chief deacon (in the East), and the congregation was bidden to pray. All prayed silently on their knees for a while; then on the signal being given, they rose from their knees, and the officiant summed up the petitions of all in a brief collect. They knelt to pray as individuals, but the corporate prayer of the church is a priestly act, to be done in the priestly posture for prayer, standing. Therefore all, not the celebrant only, rose for the concluding collect. (page 42)

This "people's prayer" derives from the profound awareness that the early church had of being the body of Jesus Christ. Unfortunately, this approach to prayer began to fade away in the fifth century and became nonexistent by the medieval period. Prayer became increasingly clericalized, with the people having no more part than an "amen" here and there. Neither did the Reformers or the Puritans recapture this sense of a people's prayer. Rather, they kept the prayers of the church in the control of the minister by means of the pastoral prayer. This has begun to change as a result of liturgical scholarship and the renewed sense of worship as rightfully being the work of the entire congregation.

In the liturgical church today, the people's prayer has been revived through the development of a number of different forms. Below is an example from Episcopal worship in which the leader and people pray responsively. Sometimes in addition to the people's answer, time is given for extemporaneous prayer by individuals:

Father, we pray for your holy Catholic Church;
That we all may be one.
Grant that ever member of the Church may truly and humbly serve you;
That your Name may be glorified by all people.
We pray for all bishops, priests, and deacons;
That they may be faithful ministers of your Word and Sacraments.
We pray for all who govern and hold authority in the nations of the world;
That there may be justice and peace on the earth.

Give us grace to do your will in all that we undertake;
That our works may find favor in your sight.
Have compassion on those who suffer from any grief or trouble;
That they may be delivered form their distress.
Give to the departed eternal rest;
Let light perpetual shine upon them.
We praise you for your saints who have entered into joy;
May we also come to share in your heavenly kingdom.
Let us pray for our own needs and those of others.
(Silence)

THE PRAYERS OF THE PEOPLE IN THE FREE CHURCH TRADITION

The ancient approach of the people's prayer may be used in the free church tradition through the bidding prayer. The minister may use the following form:

Minister: I bid you to pray for the sick.
People: (Extemporaneous prayers are offered.)
Minister: I bid you to pray for the needs of the world.
People: (Extemporaneous prayers are offered.)
Minister: I bid you to pray for the church—both the church universal and this local church.
People: (Extemporaneous prayers are offered.)
Minister: I bid you to confess your sin (when the Lord's Supper is celebrated).
People: (A unison prayer may be provided or people may confess in silence.)

The minister may close this time of prayer with a summary prayer that brings together the petitions of the people.

Some may fear this approach to prayer, arguing that "people will not pray." That is a legitimate concern. Some churches have introduced the people's prayer only to have the people stand in silence.

One way to get the people involved is to prime the pump, so to speak. Choose a dozen or more people in the church and ask them to prepare a short "extemporaneous" prayer for one of the areas of prayer. This works. For example, ask a person to mention one matter under "the needs of the world." That person will choose one subject—for example, racism—and spend the week watching for news on TV, in the newspaper, and in national magazines, just to make a brief sentence prayer. Thus, that person will have prayed for that one matter all week long. This approach to prayer can get a number of people involved and can turn the prayers of the people into true congregational prayer.

CONCLUSION

Focus on these prayer ideas and others that you may hear of or think of yourself to make the time of prayer in worship more prayerful and more participatory. Worship is not something done to us or for us, but by us. And what is true of worship in general is true of prayer specifically. Become involved in all the prayers by attentive listening and in the prayers of the people by active personal involvement. In this way, you will break through the barriers of passive worship and continually renew your relationship with God.

STUDY GUIDE

Read Session 10, "Prayer That Involves the Congregation,"
before starting the study guide.

PART I: PERSONAL STUDY

Answer the following questions on your own.

1. *Life Connection*

◆ Think back over your life in the church. Was there a worship setting in which an unusual approach was taken to prayer—a prayer time that involved the entire congregation? Describe that memory. _____

_____

_____

_____

_____

_____

_____

_____

2. *Thought Questions*

◆ Analyze the prayer of invocation (pg. 94) by writing down those parts of the prayer that speak to the following categories. Then take some time to mediate on the prayer and let God speak to you.

An ascription to God _____

_____

_____

The knowledge God has of the worshiper _____

_____

_____

The petition_____

_____

_____

The outcome _____

_____

The concluding words _____

_____

_____

_____

◆ Analyze the collect for the first Sunday after Christmas by writing down those parts of the prayer that speak to the categories listed below. Then take some time to meditate on the prayer in a manner of spiritual reading.

The ascription to God _____

_____

What God has done _____

_____

The petition _____

_____

The closing doxological statement _____

_____

◆ Analyze the prayer of confession by writing down those parts of the prayer that speak to the categories listed below. Then take some time to meditate on the prayer and make your own confession.

The ascription to God _____

The confession as to its extent of sin against God

a. _____

b. _____

c. _____

d. _____

e. _____

The attitude of the penitent _____

_____

The reason for forgiveness _____

_____

The petition _____

_____

The result of forgiveness (for the penitent) _____

_____

The result of forgiveness (for God) _____

_____

_____

• Use your own words to describe the people's prayer. _____

_____

_____

_____

_____

_____

• What are some reasons that people are reluctant to pray in public?

_____

_____

_____

_____

_____

• Deriving your cue from the people's prayer of the *Book of Common Prayer* and the suggested form for a free church, prepare a form for the people's prayer that could be used in your local church. _____

_____

_____

_____

_____

_____

_____

3. *Application*

♦ Use your own words to rewrite the prayer of invocation. Express the ideas in the prayer for use in a free church tradition.

_____

_____

_____

_____

_____

♦ Use your own words to rewrite the collect for the Sunday after Christmas. Express the ideas in the prayer for use in a free church tradition.

_____

_____

_____

_____

♦ Use your own words to rewrite the confession of sin. Express the ideas in the prayer for use in the free church tradition. _____

_____

_____

_____

_____

PART II: GROUP DISCUSSION

Write all of the group members' answers to the questions in each section on a chalkboard or flip chart.

1. *Life Connection*

♦ Begin the group discussion by asking several members of the group to share an experience of worship that included an unusual congregational prayer.

2. *Thought Questions*

♦ Talk through the parts of the invocation and explore with the class how each part of the prayer inspired them to pray.

♦ Talk through the collect for the Sunday after Christmas and explore with the class how each part of the prayer inspired them to pray.

♦ Talk through the confession of sin and explore specific references to which each part of the prayer may refer.

♦ Discuss the prayer of the people and explore why people are reluctant to pray in public.

3. *Application*

♦ Have each person present the invocation that he or she wrote. Then write a composite prayer of invocation from individual contributions. Finally, explore the spiritual meaning of each part of the prayer by asking each person to share what each part of the prayer means to him or her.

♦ Do the same as above for the collect for the first Sunday after Christmas.

♦ Do the same as above for the prayer of confession.

♦ Explore the people's prayer by asking: (a) What do you think of the idea? (b) Why do people feel reluctant to pray out loud in worship? (c) How can this church successfully introduce the people's prayer into our worship?

♦ Prepare a composite people's prayer. Conclude your study by praying the prayer.

PREACHING THAT INVOLVES THE CONGREGATION

A Study in Communicating the Word

One of the most distinguishing marks of Christian worship is preaching. I hesitate to think of how many sermons I have heard in my own lifetime. In addition to being reared in a Christian home (a preacher's kid, at that) where regular church attendance three times a week was the norm, I was also educated in a Christian college and three seminaries where regular chapel was required. I have taught in the setting of a Christian college and graduate school since 1960. Consequently, I think it is fair to say that I have heard anywhere from six to ten thousand sermons in my lifetime. That's a lot of sermons!

Most of the sermons I've heard were preached *at* me. That is to say, I entered worship with no previous idea or preparation for the sermon. I had nothing to say about the text or the theme of the sermon. I had no direct or even indirect connection with the preparation of the sermon and nothing to say in response to the sermon once it was preached.

While this is certainly the norm in most churches, it doesn't have to be. In this session we will look the sermon—how it can remain a central and important part of worship and how the congregation can become involved in its preparation and delivery.

THE CLERICALIZATION OF THE SERMON

The sermon, which originated in the Hebrew tradition, had a central place in the synagogues of the first century and played an important part in the beginning of Christianity. A cursory reading of the book of Acts introduces us to the preaching content of Peter, Paul, and Stephen and clearly demonstrates that the Christian message was spread through the proclamation of preaching.

Following the New Testament period there were very few preachers and leaders of the stature of the New Testament disciples. Research into these centuries suggests that preaching in the villages and hamlets of the Roman Empire was not at all similar to what we understand as preaching today.

The picture of preaching in the first several centuries is something like this: a lay person recognized by the community would read Scripture, make a few comments, then engage in conversation with the congregation concerning the text and the Christian faith and living in general. These questions and answers were more like an informal conversation. Preachers had not developed the science of sermon preparation or execution. This kind of sermon probably continued into the fourth and fifth century, even as the science of preaching was being developed in the city-centers of faith. Once the more rational and scientific approach to preaching had developed, the conversational homily of the rural areas died out and preaching became the sole property of the trained preacher. Preaching had been taken away from the people and clericalized.

To fully understand this development in preaching, we need to keep in mind the growth of the church and the shift in the worship setting. What began as a small group of people meeting in a house church developed into thousands of people meeting in large basilicas, necessitating the growth of theater in worship. In small intimate groups the conversational sermon fit well. When the church setting became large, it demanded a sermon more similar to the kind we all are used to hearing. But this kind of sermon can be made more intimate and personal.

GETTING THE LAITY INVOLVED

There is a trend in the church today to break the tradition of clericalized sermons and return preaching to the people. Let's look at some of the ways in which that is happening.

A small church that is struggling to survive has a special opportunity for intimacy. It simply doesn't make sense for the small church to pattern its worship after the large church. The small church can create an intimate space where people gather in an informal way to sing, to read Scripture, to pray, and to engage in a sermon conversation. Imagine forty or so people sitting in a circle or facing each other in rows that allow for conversation. Imagine the leader, an ordained person or a gifted and called lay person, reading the Scripture and then simply but powerfully engaging in a conversation with the people about the text—its meaning and its implication for Christian faith and practice!

In a large church, an intimate gathering of a small group of people obviously is not possible. Can people in this setting get involved in the sermon? The answer is yes. Let's look how congregational involvement can be accomplished in the larger church, and at methods that a number of churches are already using.

FORMING A TEXT STUDY GROUP

Most pastors conduct Bible study groups during the week. This group can study the sermon text together with the pastor each week *before* the sermon will be preached. The study can be a small, informal conversational group that explores the text for its meaning and implications. In this setting the pastor may gain new insights into the text from the experiences and questions brought to the text by the interested lay person. For these people the sermon will take on a new meaning.

Here are some other ways to involve the people in the sermon:

* Study the sermon text in Sunday school. The pastor or someone else (preferably a layperson) uses the Sunday school hour to read and study the text. Those who attend will enter worship and preaching with a more intense participation and sense of expectancy.
* Integrate the texts into personal worship during the week. Each week the pastor publishes the text of the sermon for the following week. By urging people to read and study the text during the week as part of their personal devotions, the pastor will tie together personal devotions and sermon listening. This will raise the people's involvement significantly.
* Introduce the talk-back sermon. When the pastor completes the sermon, the people are asked to "talk back" by turning to one or two persons seated near them and respond to what they have heard, felt, and experienced (note the use of affective terminology rather than cerebral terms such as "understand" or "think"). These talk-back sermons should not be used every week but may be appropriate once a month.
* Form a sermon response group. A sermon response group meets after worship (at the coffee hour) or during the week to discuss the implications of the sermon for life.

A RETURN TO CUSTOM

While some of the suggestions advanced in this session may seem a little bit strange, they are so only because we have so thoroughly clericalized the sermon that it is the only model we know. Those who may be threatened or put off by sermons that involve the congregation should remember that clericalized sermons were not the norm of the early church. It is also helpful to know that in the seventeenth and eighteenth centuries, Protestant worship sermons were almost always followed by congregational discussion. It was the custom for the minister to leave the pulpit after the sermon and stand behind the Communion table where a discussion of the sermon was conducted with the entire congregation. This practice was swept away by the introduction of revivalistic worship in the nineteenth century, a worship that emphasized evangelistic preaching. Today, most churches stress instructive and Christian living preaching. For this reason, the return of congregational involvement is imperative.

STUDY GUIDE

Read Session 11, "Preaching That Involves the Congregation,"
before starting the study guide.

PART I: PERSONAL STUDY

Answer the following questions on your own.

1. *Life Connection*

♦ Take some time to reflect on the most significant sermon you ever heard. When was it given? What was significant about it? How did it affect you personally? _____

_____

_____

_____

♦ Have you ever been personally involved as a layperson in a sermon that allowed you a special kind of input, immediate response, or post-sermon group discussion? Write about that experience. _____

_____

_____

_____

_____

2. *Thought Questions*

♦ The first recorded sermon of the early church is Peter's sermon at Pentecost in Acts 2:14–36. Describe the response to this sermon (see Acts 2:37–42). _____

_____

_____

_____

_____

_____

- One of the most important sermons of the early church was preached by Stephen (Acts 7:1–53). Describe the listeners' response to this sermon (Acts 7:54–60). _____

  _____

  _____

  _____

  _____

- Describe the listeners' response to Philip's sermon at Samaria (Acts 8:5–8).

  _____

  _____

  _____

  _____

  _____

- How did sermons change after the New Testament period and through the second century? _____

  _____

  _____

  _____

  _____

  _____

- What is meant by the clericalization of the sermon? _____

  _____

  _____

  _____

  _____

- How and why does the sermon in the small church differ from the sermon in the larger church? _____

  _____

  _____

  _____

  _____

+ Draw a space designed for intimacy of conversation for a small church in the space below.

3. *Application*

+ Explain each of the following approaches to returning the sermon to the people in the larger church:

The text study group_____

_____

Studying the sermon text in Sunday school_____

_____

Integrating texts into personal worship during the week_____

_____

The talk-back sermon _____

_____

The post-sermon response group _____

_____

+ How would the congregation of which you are a part receive the declericalization of the sermon?_____

_____

_____

_____

_____

_____

_____

PART II: GROUP DISCUSSION

Write all of the group members' answers to the questions in each section on a chalkboard or flip chart.

1. *Life Connection*

- Begin your group discussion by asking people to tell stories about their most memorable sermon.

- Continue the study by asking group members to relate any situations in which they were involved in sermon preparation or sermon response.

2. *Thought Questions*

- Take some time to discuss the following responses to sermons:

   Peter's Pentecost sermon (Acts 2:37–42)

   Stephen's sermon (Acts 7:54–60)

   Philip's sermon (Acts 8:5–8)

- Ask the members to share the space they designed for small church worship.

- Ask each person to respond to this question: What advantages and disadvantages do you see to conversation sermons in small church settings?

- Identify the advantages and disadvantages of the clericalized sermons in the larger church.

- How would you personally respond to each of the following ways of declericalizing the sermon? How would others respond? How would the pastor respond? Discuss.

   A text study group

   Studying the sermon text in Sunday school

   Integrating texts into personal worship during the week

   A talk-back sermon

   A post-sermon response group

3. *Application*

♦ Form an on-the-spot text study group. Ask the pastor to give you the texts for next Sunday's sermon. Discuss the meaning and application of the text in preparation for next Sunday's service.

♦ Respond to the sermon from this past Sunday. What did you hear, feel, and experience in the sermon? How does this sermon affect your life?

♦ Bring a recording of a recent sermon to class. Listen to part of it and experiment with a talk-back sermon. How did this sermon speak to you?

♦ Ask for the texts for next week's worship. Take these texts home with you and read and meditate on them as a spiritual discipline. Discuss how this discipline affected your listening, understanding, and application of the sermon (this particular application will need to be spread out over two studies).

SINGING THAT INVOLVES THE CONGREGATION

A Study in Congregational Song

 This past week I had two experiences of singing in worship that cover the spectrum from very poor to very strong.

My first and positive experience was at Northern Baptist Theological Seminary where I teach in the doctoral program. I taught a one-week intensive course that meets for more than forty hours, listening to lectures and doing practicum worship. The singing in this group was simply superlative. I can only describe it as an experience of singing before the throne of God with angels, archangels, cherubim, seraphim, and the whole company of saints joining in the eternal song. There were two reasons for this—the singing ability of the students and outstanding piano accompaniment. The pianist provided leadership that was strong, energetic, and pulsating with life. Consequently, the singing was uplifting and empowering.

My other experience was at Wheaton College, where I teach full-time. Every year we have special services. This year our spiritual emphasis week included both a speaker and a worship leader. The worship leader is an internationally known dance and movement leader—a man with powerful leadership skills. The morning chapel was full of life because of the strong piano leadership. But in the evening a person with excellent piano skills, but no congregational leadership skills, accompanied the congregational singing, as well as a group of dancers with banners. The singing experience was the complete opposite of the one described above. The piano tempo and sound were similar to the lounge music in a good restaurant. It was the kind of music for conversation, or better yet, to go to sleep by. Consequently, the singing was slow, lacking in energy or enthusiasm. The accompanying dance and movement, imprisoned by the slow pace of the music, fell short of the expressiveness that the leader was capable of giving it. Worship was a downer. It was dead and lacking in spiritual energy.

The point, of course, is clear. Congregational song is important to worship. When it is slow and lacking in involvement, it can depress worship. (There are times when a slow-paced song is appropriate. Even a slow song, when done right, has an energy and quality of strength about it that is similar to a more fast-paced song.)

In this study, we are going to address the role of music and congregational song in worship. How can we bring energy, spirit, and vitality to our worship through music and congregational singing?

How to Improve Congregational Hymn Singing

In recent years, hymn singing has fallen upon hard times. There was a time when every church had a hymnbook, but today that is no longer true. Thousands of "younger churches" (those that have emerged since 1970) know nothing about the hymnology of the church. Instead, the people only sing choruses projected on a screen. However, there is a move among these churches as they mature to learn more of the great hymns of the church.

So how do you introduce new hymns to churches that already use the hymnbook and to churches that have no hymnbooks?

To introduce new hymns effectively, you have to think about both words and music. The people need to become familiar with the words and the meaning of the ideas; they also need to become familiar with the tune and the actual singing of the song. How do you do it?

First, some suggestions on learning the words. Print the text in the bulletin so people can become familiar with the content as preparation for worship. Have the congregation read the words out loud at a moment in worship. Ask the people to take the words of the text and meditate on them in personal worship during the week.

John Wesley, the leader of the evangelical awakening of the nineteenth century and a prolific hymn writer, wrote about singing intelligently. "Have an eye for God in every word you sing. Aim at pleasing him more than yourself or any other creature. In order to do this, attend strictly to the sense of what you sing, and see that your heart is not carried away with the sound, but offered to God continually . . ."

Second, some suggestions on learning the tune. Most people in the pew cannot read music. Having the organist play through the song once while everyone listens isn't an adequate way to learn the music. Furthermore, stopping the flow of worship to learn a new tune is jarring to the worship sensibilities and not advisable. So the first matter is to address the when and where of learning new hymns.

The best setting is the informal atmosphere of a weekly study group, or an informal hymn singing conference or workshop. But if the majority of people present at a Sunday service are not at one of these special occasions, then the Sunday setting will be best.

Many churches take time *before* the worship begins to teach new music. This is highly appropriate even in the most formal of churches. It should be done in a manner in keeping with the tone of worship. If the worship is dignified and formal, learning new music can be done in a way that reflects that dignity and formality. If the atmosphere is casual and informal, then new hymns can be introduced in a more casual way. Here are some suggestions for this setting:

- Have the organist or pianist play the song through one time.
- Have the choir or worship team sing the song as the people listen and hum the tune.
- Take a moment to point out repetitions in the melody. Sing the repetitive part.
- Point out the lines of music that differ from the repetitive lines.
- Sing one stanza with strong leadership from the choir or worship team.

One final suggestion. Be sure to have good organ or piano leadership! Remember my opening observations.

How to Involve the Congregation in Responsorial Psalm Singing

Singing psalms in a responsorial way has made a recent return to the church. I remember as a boy the weekly responsorial reading of the psalm, but I have no recollection of psalm singing from those days of forty or fifty years ago.

But responsorial psalm singing is not a new or innovative approach to the psalms by any means. Singing the psalms antiphonally or in a responsorial way goes back to Hebrew worship and to the early church. Today's psalm singing is simply a recovery of an ancient and firmly established tradition.

In Hebrew and early Christian worship, the psalm was sung between Scripture readings. The theological conviction that stood behind placing the psalm after a Scripture reading was an understanding of worship as proclamation and response. Scripture reading is the proclamation of God; the psalm is the response of the people.

Today in the fourfold pattern of worship the responsorial psalm remains between Scripture readings. In many churches that use a contemporary song as part of their acts of entrance, psalms express the longing of the heart as the tempo quiets to a place of intimate relationship with God.

A good general rule for the use of the responsorial psalm that involves the congregation is to divide the psalm into its natural parts (at a period or the end of a thought). During worship, a reader may read the psalm, or a cantor or choir sing it, with the congregation singing the refrain or chorus of a familiar hymn at each break.

How to Involve the Congregation in Praise Songs

Praise songs have been introduced by the charismatic and the praise and worship traditions. The singing of praise songs in worship can be a very moving experience, making the congregation vulnerable to the work of the Holy Spirit. Praise music may be used to increase congregational participation in several ways:

+ Use meditative singing to help people enter into an intimate relationship with God. While the instrumentalists play a simple and low key progression, invite the congregation to sing a favorite Scripture softly, making up their own tune. This kind of singing may take place at the end of the entrance, after the sermon, or during the reception of bread and wine.
+ Use intercession singing to help people pray. Allow the musicians to play prayerful music. As they do so, encourage the congregation to call out the names of those who need healing or to pray brief words of intercession for the world and the church. Use these songs during the people's prayer.
+ Use deliverance singing to help people pray for deliverance from bondage for themselves and for others. As the musicians play music, particularly songs of Christ as victor over the powers of evil, encourage the congregation to pray for those who need deliverance from things like alcohol, permissive sex, drugs, gossip, etc. These songs may be used at the time of the people's prayer or even after the confession of sin.
+ Use a preaching song to help people respond to the sermon. Someone from the musical staff or worship team chooses a name or statement from the pastor's sermon, puts it to music on the spot, and leads the entire congregation in singing this refrain after the sermon.

Conclusion

Music and song are among the most powerful instruments of the Spirit in worship because they are nonverbal ways of approaching mystery. A relationship with God has a highly mysterious and noncognitive side to it. Often our worship is far too cognitive and verbal. Words are important in our approach to God, but they constitute one avenue only. We need to learn how to come before God through nonverbal sound as well. By returning music and sound to the people, we invite them into a personal participatory journey of relationship with God.

STUDY GUIDE

Read Session 12, "Singing That Involves the Congregation,"
before starting the study guide.

PART I: PERSONAL STUDY

Answer the following questions on your own.

1. *Life Connection*

- Recall a worship service in which the musical leadership and congregational singing were full of vitality and energy. Describe that service and your experience of worship. _____

_____

_____

_____

_____

- Recall a worship service in which the musical leadership and congregational singing were dead and lifeless. Describe that service and your worship experience._____

_____

_____

_____

_____

2. *Thought Questions*

- If you have a hymnbook at home or can borrow one from the church, leaf through it and decide what percentage of the hymns you know.
  ❑ 10–30% ❑ 31–50% ❑ 51–75% ❑ 76–100%

- If you are in a contemporary church that sings choruses most of the time, how many hymns do you know?
  ❑ fewer than 10   ❑ 10–25   ❑ 26 or more

- If you are in a church that is hymnbook oriented, how well do you know current choruses?
  ❑ Not at all   ❑ A handful   ❑ Many   ❑ I am current with new materials.

- How have new hymns or songs been introduced into the worship of your church? _____

  _____

  _____

  _____

  _____

- Summarize, in your own words, the suggestions for introducing new hymns and songs into your worship. _____

  _____

  _____

  _____

  _____

  _____

- How often does your church sing psalms in a responsorial or antiphonal manner?
  ❑ Never   ❑ Sometimes   ❑ Frequently   ❑ Regularly

- When did psalm singing originate? _____

  _____

- Where do responsorial psalms fit in worship? _____

  _____

- How may you approach psalm singing? _____

  _____

- How often does your church sing praise songs?
  ❑ Never   ❑ Sometimes   ❑ Frequently   ❑ Regularly

- When are praise songs sung?
  ❑ In the acts of entrance   ❑ In the service of the word
  ❑ At Communion   ❑ Other _____

◆ Use your own words to describe meditative singing. _____

_____

_____

_____

_____

_____

_____

_____

◆ Use your own words to describe intercession singing. _____

_____

_____

_____

_____

_____

_____

_____

_____

◆ Use your own words to describe deliverance singing. _____

_____

_____

_____

_____

_____

_____

_____

◆ Use your own words to describe the preaching song. _____

_____

_____

_____

_____

_____

_____

_____

3. *Application*

• If you have a hymnbook, teach yourself a new hymn and spend some time thinking about how you would teach this hymn to your congregation. Summarize your thoughts. _____

_____

_____

_____

_____

_____

• Read Psalm 150. Divide it into paragraphs according to its thought pattern. Choose a chorus or a refrain from a familiar hymn or song. Take time to lay out the entire psalm in a responsorial manner. After you have completed this assignment, sing it. _____

_____

_____

_____

_____

_____

_____

_____

_____

• To the best of your ability, create a meditative song. Describe the background music and the words you would match to the sound. Describe your creation. _____

_____

_____

_____

_____

_____

_____

- To the best of your ability, develop a setting for intercessory prayer for your church. _____

  _____

  _____

  _____

- Develop a setting for a deliverance song. Describe its use in your church.

  _____

  _____

  _____

  _____

- To the best of your ability, prepare a preaching song for your local church. Describe it. _____

  _____

  _____

  _____

  _____

PART II: GROUP DISCUSSION

Write all of the group members' answers to the questions in each section on a chalkboard or flip chart.

1. *Life Connection*

- Ask the group to describe a service characterized by strong musical leadership and involvement that was full of vitality and energy.

- Ask the group to describe a service that was dry, dead, and lacking in spirit.

2. *Thought Questions*

- Ask, "How familiar are you with the hymns of the church from the hymnbook?" Get a show of hands in the following categories:
  ❏ Not at all   ❏ Somewhat   ❏ Fairly familiar   ❏ Very familiar

- Ask, "How familiar are you with contemporary choruses?"
  ❏ Not at all   ❏ Somewhat   ❏ Fairly familiar   ❏ Very familiar
- Ask people to share their thoughts on introducing new hymns. What difficulties might they experience in introducing new hymns?
- Ask how people would introduce responsorial singing.
- How would their church respond to meditative singing?
- How would it respond to intercession singing?
- How would it respond to deliverance singing?
- How would it respond to the preaching song?

3. *Application Questions*
- Ask one of the members of the class to teach a new hymn. Evaluate the procedure.
- Ask one of the members of the class to teach Psalm 150, using an antiphonal method. Evaluate.
- Ask a member of the class to teach a meditative song. Evaluate.
- Ask a member of the class to teach and lead the group in intercessory prayer. Evaluate.
- Ask a member of the class to teach and lead a deliverance song. Evaluate.
- Ask a member of the class to teach and lead in a preaching song. Evaluate.

PLANNING WORSHIP THAT INVOLVES THE CONGREGATION
A *Study in the Planning of Worship*

 I have found that planning worship with a group of people can be both stimulating and challenging as well as frustrating and dis-couraging. Let me give you an example.

Occasionally I do weekend retreats for a church community. I speak about worship on Friday night and several times on Saturday, then lead a service of worship on Sunday.

Because I don't like to force my agenda on a group of people, I always ask for volunteers to help plan the worship. I make sure to announce my need for people with musical and artistic talent, as well as people who simply like to be involved in worship planning. I'm always pleasantly surprised by the numbers of people who show up for the planning meeting.

Our planning meeting usually starts with the Scripture texts that I have chosen. Sometimes someone else wants a different text, but usually the group allows us to keep the texts that reflect the theme of the retreat. Our next step is to discuss the texts. What, we ask, do these texts say to us? After a theme has emerged, we plan the structure of the acts of entrance, discussing such things as the kind of music and arts we will use. Then we plan the service of the word, paying careful attention to matters of communication. How can we communicate the word best? Should we use drama, storytelling, talk-back sermon? What kind of music should be sung between the readings? Should we use a responsorial psalm, Scripture choruses, a dance accompaniment? Next we turn to the matter of the Eucharist. Generally, the group will allow me to suggest a pattern of Eucharistic prayer, since they are unfamiliar with it. But we need to discuss the Communion music. What songs of death, then resurrection, then exaltation should we sing? And should we anoint with oil? Finally, we address the sending forth. How should the people be blessed?

What song will give them the sense of being commissioned to do the work of the Lord?

As you are reading about this, you may be thinking, Wow, sounds complicated! or, How can you ever get a large group to agree? or, Planning worship sounds like a worship experience itself.

All of these thoughts are true. That's why planning worship with members of the congregation can be both frustrating and exhilarating. It's frustrating because you always feel there are too many chiefs and not enough Indians. But planning worship with others is exhilarating because of the enthusiasm, the insights, and the creativity that emerge.

Keep in mind that worship planning is slightly different in each tradition. For example, in the liturgical tradition, which has a fairly fixed liturgy and uses weekly texts from the lectionary, you already have a considerable amount of planning done for you. In the free church tradition, where weekly change is expected, the planners may be primarily people related to music and the arts. In these churches, planning may be more demanding because the actual form and text of worship are open to more continual change. But whatever your church tradition, you will find the material that follows to be helpful.

PLANNING WORSHIP WITH THE LAITY

The purpose of including the laity in planning worship is to incorporate their input and creativity into the corporate worship of the local church. The byproduct of planning with the laity is that the worship will be *owned* by them. So how do you do it?

Let's begin with the planning team. Who should serve and how long should they serve? It is obvious that only those who have an interest in and commitment to worship should serve. The people who generally fall into this category are people with either musical or communication skills. People who have a commitment to servanthood may also find a special place on the team. Because you do not want this team to be too large or to serve for a long period of time, you may find it best to function with a number of people on a revolving-door basis. Perhaps certain persons will be appointed for a full year, while other people may serve for only part of the year. You would, for example, have some people who serve during the Christmas and Easter cycle (planning for December into June) and others for the after-Pentecost cycle (planning from June into November).

How should a planning meeting be conducted? Here are some simple steps to follow:

+ Step 1: Begin with the Scripture texts. Read them aloud. Have several versions handy. Discuss the meaning of the texts.
+ Step 2: Allow a theme to emerge. As the discussion of the texts proceeds, several possible themes will emerge. The group will eventually settle on one.
+ Step 3: Explore the place and use of music. Once the theme is clear, then the music will fall into place. Since the mood of the entrance (joyful), the word (meditative), the table (celebrative), and the dismissal (mission) differ, the content and sound of the music will change as well. The committee needs to keep this in mind.
+ Step 4: Explore the use of the arts. Artistic people who are involved in the planning stage will want to discuss the procession and recession, the possible use of drama or storytelling, and the matter of visuals in the environmental setting of worship. The question will be, What can we do to make this a space that reflects the theme (this will be especially true for seasons of the Christian year) and how can we best communicate the word of God through the Scripture readings and presentations?
+ Step 5: Prepare the prayers of worship. Usually the pastor prepares the prayers. In a church where the lay people are well trained, they may be encouraged to become involved in prayer preparation and leadership. In the ancient tradition, a deacon or lay person always led the prayers. A return to that practice is growing in the church.

We now have to consider the role of the pastor and the musical staff of the church in the planning of worship. If we are truly serious about returning worship to the people and breaking through the barriers of passive worship, we must make certain that laity input and involvement in worship planning is authentic. To achieve this authentic involvement, the pastor, the worship leader, and the staff musicians need to play a particular role.

Pastors should not be "out of the loop" on worship planning. Some pastors turn worship planning over to the worship leader or team entirely, essentially saying, Let me know if you want me to do anything other than preach. Other pastors do the opposite and exert such control that the input of the worship team or committee is unimportant. Both approaches are mistakes. Even if the pastor has given responsibility for worship leadership over to the worship leader or team, the pastor still has two very important functions. The first is a "presence-function." Just being there, responding and interacting with the proceedings, providing insight from experience, and asking crucial questions is important. The second role of the pastor is that of teacher. The pastor may give instruction about worship, drawing from biblical, historical, and theological knowledge.

What is the role of the paid musicians? Whether they are full-time or part-time, their involvement in worship planning needs to be marked by sensitivity. A musician, like a pastor, needs to learn the art of listening to the people. The people know what touches them, what makes them vulnerable, and what is performance and not ministry. Consequently, the music staff must listen. But the music staff is also called to educate. Their lifelong pursuit of music and the arts gives them knowledge and experience that a layperson does not have.

When the pastor and the worship staff become both listeners and teachers, there is an enormous benefit. Their isolation from the people is minimized; the feedback that comes from the people is maximized; and the overall effectiveness of worship as an act of praise to God and as a means through which God brings healing to the community of worship is intensified. When worship is improved, it energizes the spirit of joy and love, and the community grows enormously.

STUDY GUIDE

*Read Session 13, "Planning Worship That Involves the Congregation,"
before starting the study guide.*

PART I: PERSONAL STUDY

Answer the following questions on your own.

1. *Life Connection*
* Have you ever had the experience of planning worship—either in a group or by yourself? Summarize your experience._____

_____

_____

_____

_____

_____

* If you have not had the experience of planning worship, comment on any experience that you have had of working with a group to plan another kind of event. What were the advantages of planning *with a group* as opposed to planning the event yourself? _____

_____

_____

_____

_____

_____

2. *Thought Questions*
* Why is it important to involve the laity in planning worship? _____

_____

_____

_____

_____

_____

◆ Who should serve on a worship-planning team? _____

_____

_____

_____

_____

◆ Why is it important for the planning team to include members who serve for a long period of time and members who serve for shorter periods of time? _____

_____

_____

_____

_____

_____

◆ Use your own words to summarize the five steps of worship planning.
   1. _____
   2. _____
   3. _____
   4. _____
   5. _____

◆ Describe the role of the pastor in worship planning. _____

_____

_____

_____

_____

◆ Describe the role of the worship staff on the planning team. _____

_____

_____

_____

_____

• What are the benefits of a worship-planning team? _____

_____

_____

_____

_____

_____

3. *Application*

• Take some time to think about the actual structure of a worship-planning team. Name the roles you think are important. Then think of persons in your own church who could fill those roles. In the space below, sketch out a picture of the worship-planning team as you imagine it.

PART II: GROUP DISCUSSION

Write all of the group members' answers to the questions in each section on a chalkboard or flip chart.

1. *Life Connection*

• Begin the discussion by asking group members to share their experiences serving on a worship-planning team. What were the difficulties and the joys?

• Ask those who have served on planning teams for events other than worship to describe the value of working in team situations. The drawbacks?

2. *Thought Questions*

- What kinds of gifts and talents are available in this community that could be put to good use in a worship-planning team?

- Would you form a planning team that remained the same, a continually changing team, or a team made up of both permanent and revolving members? What is the advantage of one over the other?

- If you were the pastor, what role would you see yourself playing in the planning team?

- If you are a member of the worship or music staff, what role would you see yourself playing in the planning team?

- What benefits would accrue to your church from establishing a planning team?

3. *Application*

- Use this classroom time to actually function as a worship-planning team. Appoint people from the class to fulfill each of the roles you have imagined in this church. Then use the rest of the time to follow the five steps of preparation outlined in the text of this session.